POWER IN NUMBERS

POWER IN NUMBERS

How to Manage for Profit

BRIAN FORST

JOHN WILEY & SONS

New York / Chichester / Brisbane / Toronto / Singapore

Copyright © 1987 by Brian Forst
Published by John Wiley & Sons, Inc.

This publication is designed to provide accurate and
authoritative information in regard to the subject
matter covered. It is sold with the understanding that
the publisher is not engaged in rendering legal, accounting,
or other professional service. If legal advice or other
expert assistance is required, the services of a competent
professional person should be sought. *From a Declaration
of Principles jointly adopted by a Committee of the
American Bar Association and a Committee of Publishers.*

Library of Congress Cataloging-in-Publication Data:

Forst, Brian.
   Power in numbers.

   Bibliography: p.
   Includes index.
   1. Financial statements.   2. Corporations—Finance.
I. Title.

HG4028.B2F58   1987   658.1'51   87-21555
ISBN 0-471-62809-3

Printed in the United States of America

10 9 8 7 6 5 4 3 2 1

To my parents,
Kurt and Rosemary Forst

PREFACE

Successful businesses succeed for a variety of reasons. If one reason stands out, it is this: the people at the top have a single-minded intention to succeed—they set their goals high and then they "go for it," purposefully tracking performance and making corrective maneuvers as the need becomes apparent. People who run successful businesses learn before long that they can't track performance and guide the business effectively without good data and a profit-focused logic for analyzing the data.

Unfortunately, information about how to create really useful financial data and how to analyze the data—to the extent that it exists at all—has been inaccessible, written largely by and for accountants and professors of finance rather than managers.

The vast body of writings on the analysis of financial data has fallen short in another important respect as well. The firm's financial statements, especially the income statement and balance sheet, are treated as backward-looking report cards of business—useful primarily for presentation to banks, venture capitalists, stockholders, tax collectors, and major vendors and customers—rather than as resources that can provide a blueprint for the firm's profitability. This book presents information about how these reports can serve as power tools for improving the firm's financial future.

Power in Numbers is written for managers. It presents a straightforward approach to creating financial information that is clear and managerially useful, and it builds on and attempts to demystify the tools that are conventionally used for analyzing financial data. It aims to provide tools that will empower managers to analyze the data specifically so that the firm's profitability will be improved.

The concepts are based on procedures that work. Most successful businesses already use them, but generally learn them the hard way. This book aims to make the information available to businesses that might not otherwise discover those procedures, and to expedite the process for businesses that would eventually become profitable anyway.

A word about how to read this book. If you're like me and a lot of other readers, you often go to the summary of a book or long article before attending to the details. We do this to establish that the basic concepts make good sense before committing valuable time and energy to them, or sometimes because we feel that we already know enough about certain details and don't need to review them. Most business people check out the bottom line of the income statement before attending to the details. Chapter 14 is sort of the bottom line chapter of this book. It's all right to read that chapter first—this isn't a suspense novel. It's equally all right to read the 13 preceding chapters first.

BRIAN FORST

Reston, Virginia
August, 1987

ACKNOWLEDGMENTS

Authors are often grateful to their spouses for being so patient. I am, too; but I'm grateful to Judy, my wife and best friend, primarily for being so involved. This book would not exist were it not for her. She encouraged the project from start to finish, reviewed the drafts with care, and asked just the right questions along the way. Her coaching and willingness to put the principles of managing by the numbers to work in her own business were inspirational beyond measure.

I wish also to thank the corporate executives who gave so willingly of their time and energy to provide the case study information in Chapters 11 and 12. Special debts of gratitude are owed to Larry Hyatt, Vice President for Operations, Planning and Control of Marriott Corporation; Eugene Miller, Executive Vice President and CFO of USG Corporation; David Sykes, Treasurer and CFO of Giant Food Inc.; and to each of the chief executive officers of the small businesses interviewed for Chapter 12.

Others provided extremely helpful comments on draft manuscripts. The thoughtful remarks of Leo Blatz, Bill McKechnie, and Sharon Verdery were especially useful.

Special notes of thanks are in order, too, to Laura and Eric Forst for their diligent research assistance; to David Ungerer, my mentor in publication matters; and to Steve Kippur and Mike Hamilton of John Wiley and Sons for their strong support.

In addition, Professor Peter Drucker graciously granted permission to use for Chapter 5 his description of the strategic planning process, from *Management: Tasks, Responsibilities, Prac-*

tices (Harper & Row, 1973). Permission to quote material from annual reports was granted by Warren E. Buffet, Chairman of Berkshire Hathaway Inc., and by representatives of the Digital Equipment Corporation and the International Business Machines Corporation. Permission to use material for the quotations that introduce chapters was given by: Harold Geneen (the introductory quotes for Chapters 1 and 7 are from his *Managing*; Doubleday, 1984); Walter Wriston (the Chapters 2 and 10 introductory quotes are from *Risk and Other Four-Letter Words*; Harper & Row, 1986); and *Forbes* (the introductory quotes for Chapters 4, 8, 11, 13, 14, and 15 are reprinted from *The Forbes Scrapbook of Thoughts on the Business Life*). The introductory quotation for Chapter 6 is from *Home Book of Quotations*, published by Dodd, Mead & Company, Inc.

B.F.

CONTENTS

1

ACCUMULATING WEALTH: THE ROLE OF FINANCIAL INFORMATION

. . . thousands of businesses go bankrupt every year, hundreds of others merge or are taken over because they are in trouble, and the root of almost all of these troubled situations can be traced back to an inattention to the numbers involved.

—Harold Geneen

We live in a time of unprecedented opportunity. No era in the history of humanity has been characterized by so much wealth available to so many people. The accumulation of wealth is, of course, not the ultimate purpose of mankind, but few would care to argue with the notion that wealth allows people to achieve higher goals: contribution to others, personal enlightenment, adventure, aesthetics, and so on. We need no longer apologize for the pursuit of wealth accumulation as a means to higher ends.

How did so many people gain access to so much wealth? Largely because a spirit of enterprise has fostered a sustained and almost inconceivable rate of advance in technology. Even as recently as 1980 the idea that a high-powered computer sys-

1

tem could be purchased for less than 20 percent of the price of a modest new automobile in the latter half of the 1980s, or that people would be able to survive for long periods of time with artificial hearts, was science fiction.

The most profound technological improvements, however, have consisted not of advancements in computers and medical science; they have consisted of more subtle advancements in the way we think, the way we relate to one another, and the manner in which we conduct business. The technologies of management and human resource development, although subject to countless fads, have nonetheless advanced to levels that have stimulated the profound breakthroughs we have witnessed in science and engineering, production efficiency, and in the delivery of services. As a result of these leaps in the technologies of human relations, management, and science and engineering, more people than ever before have become aware that substantial personal wealth is attainable, bringing with it the possibility of achieving higher personal goals.

Yet, the riddle of *how* to attain wealth remains as old as mankind itself. Most people work hard at their jobs, and attempt to invest their savings prudently, as their primary means of accumulating wealth; but few are able to attain substantial wealth in that conventional way. The hard reality is that most very wealthy people were either born that way or they acquired their wealth by building a successful business enterprise.

Since most of us are not children of the super rich, we are left with one real prospect for attaining substantial wealth: build a successful business.

THE KEY TO BUSINESS SUCCESS: SOUND FINANCIAL INFORMATION

Building a successful business is not a trivial matter. It has become a widely cited statistic that about 75 percent of all new businesses in the United States do not survive for even five years. At some point, most entrepreneurs—and all good ones —become aware that creating an attractive product or service, and managing a successful business, requires more than terrific ideas about how to produce and sell. Also required is sound financial information. Much like the crew of an airplane needs accurate and relevant information to ensure that their flight destination is reached safely, quickly, and economically, the executives of a business, if they are to have some assurance of success, need accurate and relevant information to ensure that their financial destination, generally expressed in terms of profit, is reached. Sound financial information consists of accurate data regarding two questions:

1. How has the business been doing recently? and
2. Where does it stand right now?

These questions can be answered by examining two basic financial statements: the *income statement* and the *balance sheet*.

A third question is also critically important: Where is the business likely to be in the future? Well-run businesses address this question as part of the process of strategic planning, and for shorter term purposes as well, especially cash flow management and control. Although this question calls for a sort of speculation that is absent from the preparation of the income statement and balance sheet, those two statements are indispensable tools for making such projections, as will be demonstrated in Chapters 7 and 8.

The income statement and balance sheet are familiar to most business people, but they are widely viewed as a necessary evil. They are regarded by many executives as documents that are needed primarily to raise funds and for tax purposes. Banks must see the income statement and balance sheet before extending credit to the business; the Securities and Exchange Commission requires that corporations make them available to capital investors; and the Internal Revenue Service requires information from these statements for the reporting of income taxes. The firm's basic financial statements are used widely for external purposes; they are used too infrequently for management purposes.

Many popular theories of management also pay very little attention to basic financial statements as management tools. Considerably more has been written about managing by "walking around," managing by applying the recent developments in the theory of organizational behavior, and managing by following the Japanese business model, than about how to use financial data as an essential tool for the diagnosis and treatment of business ailments. Financial statements are widely regarded, first and foremost, as the report cards of business, the certificates that tell the story on the bottom line, not as instruments that are capable of providing a basis for in-depth understanding of why businesses succeed or fail.

This is not to suggest that theories of management that have more to do with organizational psychology than with financial statements are not important. Indeed, the profound importance of certain developments in the realm of the technology of human relations and organizations has already been acknowledged.

Financial statements have, in short, been largely ignored as tools for obtaining a penetrating and comprehensive understanding of the performance and condition of the business, and for providing a solid basis for directing the course of the business.

Executives can do much more with their financial reports than just have them prepared for fund-raising and tax purposes; they can do more than merely look to the bottom line of the income statement to see how their businesses are doing. These statements can be much more than bureaucratic necessities and corporate report cards.

How? By structuring the financial data of the business in a managerially useful way and then applying straightforward analytical procedures to see how the business is doing, both as a whole and in its usefully distinguishable parts—and both in the short and long run. In so doing, business executives can transform standard financial statements into indispensable management tools. This book aims to help with that transformation.

2

FINANCIAL STATEMENTS: SOME ESSENTIAL PRINCIPLES

What are we trying to do? It seems to me what we should be trying to do is to produce reliable, timely, informative data within an understandable framework that allows people to make informed judgments.

—WALTER B. WRISTON

Financial statements summarize the details of the accounting data of a business to serve a variety of important purposes. As noted in the previous chapter, they serve two primary audiences: management and persons outside the business.

The information needs of management usually differ substantially from those of persons outside the business. Managers generally need detailed information, and they need information that is aimed to the future, toward improvement. Financial statements that respond to management's needs focus on specific products, services, departments, or even individuals within the business, so that those smaller units can have tangible feedback on performance as a basis for modifying business policies and procedures, and for making decisions that will

7

improve the business. The degree of detail contained in those statements should be determined by considering both the cost of maintaining the data in such precision and the value to managers of having the detail.

Persons outside the organization typically don't need such detailed information. They do, as a rule, want assurance that the information they see is consistent with generally accepted accounting principles (accountants use the acronym GAAP). Outsiders usually review the business's financial statements primarily to examine the overall health of the business or to satisfy specific interests: A lending agent looks to see how much risk is present in extending a loan to the business; a stockholder or other investor may care to examine only the income statement to see how much profit was made last year; a prospective client may wish to look at the balance sheet to see how much of the firm's capitalization is in the form of equity before entering into a large contract with it; a labor union official may wish only to see how profitable the company has been and how management's compensation has risen relative to labor's; an IRS agent will scrutinize only those financial statement items that show up on the business's tax forms; and so on. These various groups, while often deeply concerned about the future of the business, nonetheless tend to adopt more of a backward looking orientation than does management.

FINANCIAL PERFORMANCE AND FINANCIAL CONDITION

Regardless of their purpose, financial statements reflect two quantifiable aspects of a business: its *financial performance* and its *financial condition*. Performance relates to how the business operates over a period of time; condition relates to how the business stands at a point in time.

The primary statement of financial performance is the *income statement*. Sometimes called the profit and loss statement or the statement of operations, the income statement documents the revenues, cost directly associated with revenues, and other costs of the business over a specified period. The income statement is discussed in depth in Chapter 4.

The ubiquitous term *bottom line*, which has come into popular colloquial use to refer to the ultimate result of virtually any human endeavor, actually derives from the last line on the income statement. The last line reports the company's net income or profit, the most basic measure of the financial performance from the operations of the business over a year or portion of a year.

The primary statement of the financial condition of a business is its *balance sheet*. (The balance sheet is in fact often called the statement of financial condition.) It provides potentially useful information about the assets, liabilities, and equities (or net worth) of a business. That report, divided into two parts, derives its name from the fact that one part is in balance with the other part. Specifically, the left side (sometimes it is arranged as the top part) provides details about the assets of the business; the right side (or bottom part) provides details about the liabilities and equities of the business; and the report balances because a business's total assets always equal the grand total of its liabilities plus equity. That report is described in considerable detail in Chapter 5.

Both the income statement and the balance sheet derive their data from the *general ledger*, which is the business's data base of financial transactions, organized and summarized by the individual accounts that constitute the detailed components of the business. Companies traditionally maintained their general ledgers in large ledger books with light green pages; today, all but the smallest businesses have converted to computerized systems that include general ledgers and the full range of financial reports (still available on light green paper!).

THE LINKAGE BETWEEN THE INCOME STATEMENT AND THE BALANCE SHEET

The income statement and balance sheet are tightly linked. Profits earned during a particular period that are retained by the business rather than distributed to owners or employees show up on the bottom line of the income statement as net income. On the balance sheet, those profits are added to the net worth of the business as retained earnings to yield the net worth for the end of the period. Thus, the increase (or decrease) in the net worth of a business, reported on two successive balance sheets, equals the net income (or loss) of the business during the intervening period, reported on the income statement.

These fundamental relationships are summarized algebraically in Exhibit 2-1, and graphically in Exhibit 2-2. The business's net worth is reflected on the balance sheet at an initial point in time as the difference between assets, above the line, and liabilities, below the line. The business can increase its net worth by producing net income, reflected on the bottom line of the income statement as the difference between revenues and costs, during the period of operations that follows the initial time point. The production of net income then shows up on the next balance sheet (under retained earnings) as an increase in

EXHIBIT 2-1
Three Fundamental Accounting Equations

1. *The Balance Sheet Equation:*

   $$\text{Net Worth} = \text{Assets} - \text{Liabilities}$$

2. *The Income Statement Equation:*

   $$\text{Net Income} = \text{Revenue} - \text{Costs}$$

3. *The Linkage Equation:*

   $$\text{Net Worth}_{t+1} = \text{Net Worth}_t + \text{Net Income}_t$$

EXHIBIT 2-2
How Improved Business Condition Shows Up on the Financial Statements

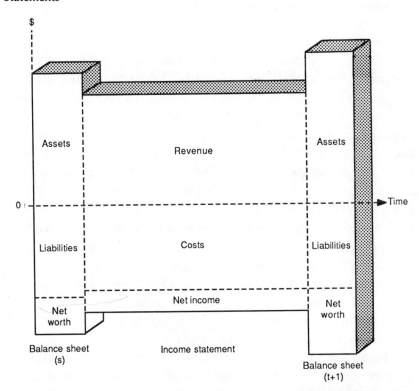

net worth and, in the example depicted in Exhibit 2-2, as an increase in assets and a decline in liabilities—the business used its profit to purchase more revenue-producing capability (assets) and reduce its debts.

WHOSE BOTTOM LINE?

Increasing the bottom line of the income statement thus permits the business to either invest in itself or reduce its debts, or both. Leaving aside until later (Chapters 5, 6, and 10) the question of which of those options is best, we can address a more basic set of issues: Is it good to produce a large bottom line amount? Why leave any income in the business at all? Why not distribute it to the principals? Isn't that why they're in business?

Income is, indeed, frequently taken out of the business by the principals, as salaries or bonuses when the principals are on the payroll, or as dividends when they're stockholders (often the paid officers and the principal stockholders are the same people). When income is left in the business, it is often taxed twice, first as business income and then, when it is later taken out either as pay or dividends, as personal income. As a result, many principals do not allow the business to grow through retained earnings. Besides, growth may not be viewed as desirable for some owners, such as those who prefer not to delegate their work to others and those who fear that if the business grows significantly they will lose control of it.

Whether earnings are retained or distributed thus depends on a variety of factors. If the principals believe that the business can produce more income with the after-corporate-tax, but before-personal-tax dollars than the principals can earn outside the business on their own with the before-corporate-tax, but after-personal-tax dollars, or if they're more interested in growth and long-term profit than in profit in the short term, they'll be inclined to leave the money in the business. On the other hand, if they're more interested in consuming than investing, or if they prefer not to expand the business, they'll be more inclined to take the money out.

So, what shows up on the bottom line is likely to depend heavily on the objectives of the principals of the business. The bottom line for an investing owner may simply be the return on equity (usually measured in terms of net profit after taxes as a percentage of equity). For the salaried owner, it may consist of net profit after taxes, plus salary and bonuses, plus perquisites. For the lender, it is likely to be interest, usually expressed as a percentage of the amount lent. To the chief financial officer, net profit is very important, but cash flow is often even more critical. The bottom line for the manager of a division, department, or other segment of the business might be the segment's operating profit as a percentage of the assets of the segment. The stockholder's bottom line is often expressed in terms of earnings per share: net profit after taxes divided by the number of shares outstanding.

In short, the bottom line of the interested party is not necessarily the bottom line on the income statement. "The bottom line," according to Edwin Herbert Land, "is in heaven."

ACCOUNTING CONVENTIONS FOR EXTERNAL REPORTS AND FOR MANAGEMENT REPORTS

The bottom line of the financial statements that are used externally may differ substantially from the bottom line of the statements that are used for management purposes. The external statements, and the accounting conventions that govern the recording of the data that make up those statements, must conform with generally accepted accounting principles (GAAP). Indeed, one of the first and foremost functions of the auditor is to assess the conformity of a business's financial statements and accounting conventions with GAAP.

As the name implies, generally accepted accounting principles are standards and conventions that guide the preparation of financial statements. A legitimate financial report is one that has been signed by a certified public accountant—signed with the stated opinion that the financial statements in the report conform to GAAP.

Where do generally accepted accounting principles come from? From a panel of high priests of the accounting profession, the Financial Accounting Standards Board, seven prominent members of the American Institute of Certified Public Accountants.

Generally accepted accounting principles do not apply to the financial statements used by management. As noted earlier, management's purposes often differ from those of persons outside the business who have special interests in its financial statements, and management is free to produce financial reports that serve its own legitimate purposes as long as its external statements conform to GAAP.

In fact, for many management purposes, the business is poorly served by GAAP. A prominent example is the accounting profession's reliance on book value rather than market value as the basis for recording assets in the general ledger, and therefore on the balance sheet. The *book value* of an asset is the original purchase cost less accumulated depreciation or amortization. That value, not the amount that is likely to be received if the asset were sold to the highest bidder, is the number that is carried in the business's general ledger and in its financial statements.

A management decision to replace an asset should be based not on its book value, but on what it will sell for, what it will cost to replace it, the respective maintenance or support costs associated with the asset and its candidate replacement, the respective revenue that the asset and its candidate replacement can be expected to generate, the firm's liquidity, and perhaps other factors. The asset's book value is not a relevant factor in this decision, except insofar as book value may have tax implications for the sale of the asset. A business that uses an asset's book value rather than either its market value or its relative revenue-producing value as the measure of the worth of the asset could end up making very unprofitable business decisions.

Yet, for external reporting purposes, the asset's book value is the only proper amount to use. The reason is simple: Until the asset is actually sold, its market value is not a known quantity.

Generally accepted accounting principles make use of known quantities, such as an asset's original cost less accumulated depreciation, rather than ones that are subject to speculation, such as an asset's market value or its projected revenue-producing value. When the asset is actually sold for cash, the difference between its book value and its sale price will show up on the income statement as a gain or loss in the sale of the asset, and on the balance sheet as the difference between the reduction in the book value of the asset and the gain in cash.

It is clear, in any case, that the accounting standards for external reports differ significantly from those for management reports. They are not always more demanding, however. In fact, the level of detail needed to provide management with the information it needs to effectively monitor and control each important aspect of the business—and to make profitable decisions—can be substantially more demanding than the level of detail required for external reporting purposes.

Obviously, detailed information tends to be more costly than aggregated information, and the details should not be created if the costs of creating and using them exceed their likely contribution to the bottom line. A primary purpose of the remainder of this book is to provide a sense of how each essential type of management information contributes to profitability.

FINANCIAL STATEMENTS: A SUMMARY OF THE ESSENTIAL PRINCIPLES

A few key points are worth restating:

> Financial statements serve a variety of useful purposes, both internally for management uses and externally for those who invest in or do business with the firm.

> The income statement gives information about the firm's financial performance over a period of time, and the balance

sheet gives information about its financial status at a point in time.

For any given period, the profits that show up on the bottom line of the income statement are equal to the increase in retained earnings reported on the balance sheets for the start and end of the period.

Financial statements used for external reporting purposes must conform to generally accepted accounting principles (GAAP); management's needs, on the other hand, are often poorly served by reports that conform to those principles.

3

SELECTING ACCOUNTING CONVENTIONS THAT REDUCE TAXES

*There is nothing sinister in so arranging one's affairs as to keep
taxes as low as possible. Everybody does so, rich or poor; and all
do right. Nobody owes any public duty to pay more than the law
demands.*

—JUSTICE LEARNED HAND

Generally accepted accounting principles (GAAP), which tend
to be less flexible than sound management principles, do nonetheless provide a considerable degree of latitude in reporting financial data. How the company's executives select among the
available options within GAAP can in fact have a profound impact on the bottom line.

The primary reason: taxes. The line just above the bottom
line on the annual income statement is Income Taxes, and
maximizing the bottom line includes the selection of accounting conventions that keep those taxes small, or that allow the
firm to pay its income taxes as late as possible. Maximizing
pretax profit in the current period is not generally equivalent to
maximizing the bottom line, because of the firm's legitimate
opportunities to reduce and to defer tax payments.

17

Obviously, it's preferable to reduce taxes than to defer them, but if tax payments can't be avoided, deferring the payments is better than paying them in the current period. Why? Because the firm can put the cash made available by the deferral to profitable uses at no interest charge. When the government offers an interest-free loan, most firms take it.

In this chapter we will discuss four sets of tax reporting choices—all fully within the domain of GAAP—that are available to businesses:

What month to select to end the fiscal year

When to report revenues and expenses

How to depreciate assets, and

How to allocate and value the inventory.

Other choices are important, too, choices that are more basic than the selection among alternative accounting conventions. For example, the form of business organization that is chosen can have a major impact on the bottom line. Whether the business is established as a proprietorship, a partnership, a corporation, or a corporation taxed as a partnership (an S corporation) is bound to affect the bottom line—largely because of the tax implications of the respective options—even though the actual workaday operations of the enterprise may be essentially unaffected by that decision. That choice can lead to more than a mere tax deferral; it can result in a legitimate reduction in the income taxes that the firm must pay.

Firms that have already been set up as dividend-paying corporations can legitimately reduce taxes in another way: replace their dividend payments, which are not tax-deductible, with interest payments, which are. Corporations that started issuing low-grade bonds in the 1980s to purchase and retire their own shares of common stock—thus replacing equity with debt— often did so primarily to reduce the risk of losing control of the company by way of a hostile takeover. As a pleasant by-product, those that had been paying dividends reduced their taxes as well. For each dollar of dividends thus converted to a dollar of interest, a corporation paying income taxes at the statutory maximum rate of 34 percent ended up with 34 cents more on the bottom line.

Selecting the form of the business organization and retiring equity can affect the firm's tax obligation, but these are not accounting conventions, like the determination of when to end the fiscal year, when to report revenues and expenses, and so on. The business cannot be fickle about this latter set of choices. Once made, federal and state regulations prohibit frequent shifts from one accounting convention to another. Specific limits on such shifts are discussed later.

WHEN TO END THE FISCAL YEAR

A year of operations for the business can end on December 31—a calendar year basis—or it can end on the last day of any other month. The choice is the chief executive officer's. A calendar year is simplest, since the alternative is to have the months of the business year straddling two calendar years.

For tax purposes, however, most firms choose not to have their business year end on December 31. The primary reason is that the operation of most businesses is seasonal; since revenues do not usually arrive precisely when expenses are incurred, the amount of the first year of income that the business reports (or any year of a growing business) can vary substantially depending on the month that is chosen to end the fiscal year. The month chosen should be the one that, over the years, defers the most taxes from each fiscal year to the next.

Once chosen, the fiscal year cannot be changed willy-nilly. The Internal Revenue Service requires a substantive business reason for the change other than a tax advantage; indeed, the

IRS may not go along with the change if a significant tax advantage results.

WHEN TO REPORT REVENUES AND EXPENSES

Most businesses report revenues when the sales transaction is closed—as indicated, for example, by the payment of a deposit or the placement of an order by a customer with an account—even when the full cash payment has not yet been received. This practice is based on the straightforward notion that it is unrealistic, in most businesses, to assume that the cash will not be paid following most orders. Because the revenue is earned, or accrues, before the cash is paid under this method of accounting, the practice is referred to as the *accrual basis*. A business that uses the accrual method applies it not only to the reporting of revenues, but also to the reporting of interest, depreciation, and other expenses that can accrue before payment is made. The accrual method is, under all circumstances, an acceptable method of accounting under GAAP.

The conventional alternative method is the *cash basis* of accounting. Under the cash method, revenues and expenses are not reported in the general ledger or the financial statements until cash passes into or out of the business. This is a more conservative approach; it assumes that a signed sales contract without full cash payment is, as far as the financial records go, earned revenue only to the extent that the customer has actually paid for the goods or services.

For many businesses, there is no opportunity to choose between the accrual and cash systems. Businesses that sell products requiring significant inventories—manufacturers, wholesalers, and retailers—generally must use the accrual method of accounting both for tax purposes and for external reporting purposes.

An alternative to the cash and accrual methods for a few businesses is a hybrid of the two.* One example, which has been called the modified cash accounting (MCA) approach, is used by some professional service partnerships, such as small and medium-size law firms, to provide a basis for allocating to partners only those profits that have been locked in.** Under the MCA approach, revenues are posted on a cash basis and expenses are posted on an accrual basis. The profits are locked in under this system in that the business adopts pessimistic assumptions both with respect to revenues (don't post them until the cash is received) and with respect to expenses (post them as soon as the *commitment is made to* purchase).

The selection among these alternative systems, for those businesses that have the choice, can have a considerable impact on taxes paid in the current period. Under the accrual system, both revenues and costs are posted early, so both reported profits and taxes tend to be higher than under the other systems.* Under the cash system, revenues and costs are posted later, so that profits and taxes tend to be lower in the current period than under the accrual system. Under the MCA hybrid approach, expenses are posted early and revenues late, so that both reported profits and taxes tend to be lower than under the other two systems. Eventually, of course, the government will get its tax money, but the firm can put the cash not paid until next year to good use in the meantime.

The ultimate selection of an alternative depends, in any event, on the nature of the business. The prudent executive

---

*Stephen F. Gertzman and Mary-Ellen Hunt, "A Basic Guide to Tax Accounting Opportunities," *Journal of Accounting* (February 1984), pp. 60-74.
**Theodore C. Frederick, "Cash or Accrual Basis Accounting," *Legal Economics* (March/April 1983), pp. 51-59.
*An important exception is the case in which a service-oriented business receives large prepayments for services to be delivered later. In many such cases, the accrual method can permit a deferral of the reporting of income for tax purposes that exceeds that available under the cash method.

should follow the advice of a knowledgeable tax lawyer or tax accountant in selecting a system for posting revenues and costs.

Businesses that do use either the cash basis or a hybrid approach for tax purposes would do well, for management purposes, to maintain a separate set of records that use the accrual system. The reason is simple: The accrual basis provides a more realistic picture of both the financial performance and condition of the business than does either the cash or most hybrid systems.

If the accrual basis seems overly optimistic with respect to revenues (a few customers end up not paying their bills), a contra account can be set up to provide a realistic reserve for revenues that eventually have to be backed out of the books because of the failure of some customers to pay. Thus, while other systems for reporting revenues may have the advantages associated with presenting a conservative earnings picture— including tax advantages—the accrual system, with reserve accounts set up based on historical experience, is likely to provide the most realistic, and therefore the most managerially useful, picture of the business's finances.

HOW TO DEPRECIATE ASSETS

An asset may have a useful life of several years, although the business typically pays for it in the year of the purchase. The expense of such an asset, its *depreciation,* is not reported fully in the year of the expenditure; instead, it is spread over the estimated life of the asset. Why? Because the asset produces value for the business throughout the productive life of the asset, hence its expense should accrue accordingly. The business can, after all, usually sell the asset after its first year of use;

to ignore that value on the balance sheet would create an unrealistically negative picture of the business's financial condition.

(Note the use of the terms *expense* and *expenditure*. Accountants use the term *expense* when a business's assets are used to produce revenue in the near term; an expense thus directly decreases income to the extent of the decline in the value of the assets used. An *expenditure* represents any payment, including the use of one asset, such as cash, to purchase another asset, such as inventory or supplies, that will produce revenue in a later period. Thus, an expenditure, unlike an expense, need not diminish income.)

Exhibit 3-1 summarizes several generally accepted procedures for spreading the costs of a long-term asset (that is, an asset with a productive life of at least one year). The simplest is the *straight-line depreciation* method: Simply divide the purchase cost of the asset by its expected life in years, and allocate that quotient into each and every year of the expected life of the asset. For assets that decline in value at approximately a constant rate, this approach is accurate as well as simple.

Most assets, however, don't decline in value at a constant rate. Most decline in value at a faster rate in the early years of their lives than in the later years. For such assets, the straight-line depreciation method produces distortions in both of the primary financial statements of the business: On the balance sheet, *book values* (i.e., the asset values that show up in the general ledger—original purchase price less accumulated depreciation) will exceed the market worth of the assets; on the income statement, depreciation costs will be artificially low, and therefore profit will be inflated. Since the Internal Revenue Service doesn't distinguish between inflated profits and uninflated ones, as long as acceptable accounting procedures are used, businesses that use the straight-line depreciation method may be paying consistently higher taxes than are required.

The usual alternative to the straight-line method is an *acceler-*

EXHIBIT 3-1
Summary of Four Standard Depreciation Methods

Method	Description	Tax/Management Effect
Straight-line method	Allocates the purchase cost of the asset equally to each year over the life of the asset.	Yields low reported costs in early years, thus high early-year profits and taxes.
Double declining balance method	The depreciation for each year is twice the straight-line percentage rate applied to the remaining book value.	Maximizes reported costs in early years, thus minimizes reported early-year profits; not for tax purposes.
Sum-of-the-years'-digits method	The depreciation rate declines each year; see text for precise formula.	Accelerates early-year costs, thus reduces reported early-year profits; not for tax purposes.
Accelerated cost recovery system	Shortens the reported life of the asset over 3-, 5-, 10-, or 15-year schedules, depending on the class of property.	Acceleration method used for tax purposes; tends to be less aggresive than other accelerated methods in early years, most aggressive over asset life.

ated depreciation method. Under accelerated depreciation, the amount of depreciation recorded in the early years of the life of an asset exceeds that recorded in the later years. One standard form of accelerated depreciation consists of reducing a long-term asset by a constant percentage of the asset's book value; the most common example of this is the *double declining balance* (DDB) method. Under DDB, the depreciation for a given year is calculated by applying twice the straight-line depreciation percentage rate to the asset's remaining book value.

Suppose, for example, that a business purchases a computer for $8000 that it plans to use for 8 to 10 years. It may, for management purposes, select an 8-year life over which to allocate the depreciation expense of the machine (if the computer ends up being used for 10 years, the business will obtain value for two years from an asset with a book value of zero; remember, book values can be misleading). Under the straight-line method, $1000 would be the depreciation amount for each of the eight years. Under the DDB method, $2000 would be the depreciation amount for the first year (twice the straight-line rate of 12.5 percent), leaving $6000 of book value; for the second year, the depreciation amount would be $1500 (25 percent of $6000); for the third year, the depreciation would amount to $1125 (25 percent of $4500); and so on.

Another common accelerated depreciation approach, the *sum-of-the-years'-digits* (SYD) method, applies a different rate each year. For our computer example, the first year's depreciation rate would be:

$$\frac{8}{1 + 2 + 3 + \ldots + 8} = 8/36,$$

which when applied to the purchase amount of $8000 gives $1778 of depreciation for the first year. For the second year we would have:

$$\frac{7}{1 + 2 + 3 + \ldots + 8} = 7/36,$$

which when applied to the original expenditure of $8000 yields $1556 of depreciation; for the third year, 6/36 of $8000 amounts to $1333; and so on.

The federal government gave us an alternative accelerated depreciation method, for tax purposes, with the Economic Recovery Tax Act of 1981. Under that Act, the cost of a long-term asset can be depreciated for tax purposes over a shorter time period than the productive life of the asset. The *accelerated cost recovery system* (ACRS) was created by the Act, allowing personal property to be depreciated over 3, 5, 10, or 15 years, depending on the class of property; for example, the Act allows business computers to be depreciated over five years and real property (buildings, not land) to be depreciated over 15 years. Under the 1981 Economic Recovery Tax Act, the ACRS replaces the use of other accelerated depreciation methods for tax purposes; these other methods, including the DDB and SYD methods, may, of course, still be used for mangement purposes. The straight-line depreciation method may still be used for tax purposes, as may longer asset lives than those specified under ACRS.

For our computer example, the applicable ACRS life is five years, and the ACRS rate for any 5-year asset is 15 percent for the first year, 22 percent for the second year, and 21 percent for each of the next three years. If our hypothetical business anticipated declining value from the machine over its projected 8-year life, it would probably choose the ACRS approach for tax purposes and one of the other depreciation methods for management purposes.

Note that the depreciation rates under ACRS are accelerated only because the presumed asset life is shortened—the rate applied to the first year is actually lower than that applied to later years, and is flat during most of the period.

How do the four methods of depreciation described above compare? The results are summarized in Exhibit 3-2. The asset is written off most quickly under ACRS and is depreciated most slowly under the straight-line depreciation method. By the end of the fifth year, the computer is fully written off under the ACRS, whereas $3000 of book value still shows up in the general ledger after five years under the straight-line method, assuming and 8-year asset life. The DDB and SYD methods, because they are accelerated with respect to the depreciation rate applied in the early years of the life of the asset rather than with respect to the presumed length of asset life, produce

EXHIBIT 3-2

Depreciation Amounts Under Four Depreciation Methods: Purchase of an $8,000 Computer with an 8-Year Life

Year	Straight-Line Method		Double Declining Balance Method		Sum-of-the-Years' Digits Method		Accelerated Cost Recovery System	
	Annual	Cum've	Annual	Cum've	Annual	Cum've	Annual	Cum've
1	$1,000	$1,000	$2,000	$2,000	$1,778	$1,778	$1,200	$1,200
2	1,000	2,000	1,500	3,500	1,556	3,333	1,760	2,960
3	1,000	3,000	1,125	4,625	1,333	4,667	1,680	4,640
4	1,000	4,000	844	5,469	1,111	5,778	1,680	6,320
5	1,000	5,000	633	6,102	889	6,667	1,680	8,000
6	1,000	6,000	475	6,576	667	7,333		8,000
7	1,000	7,000	356	6,932	444	7,778		8,000
8	1,000	8,000	267	7,199	222	8,000		8,000
Total	$8,000		$7,199		$8,000		$8,000	

higher depreciation costs than the ACRS in the early years, but lower costs in the middle years. From a tax standpoint, ACRS depreciation tends to maximize aftertax income for a business that reports profits in the early years of the life of an asset. For management purposes, however, the best system to use is that which most closely depicts reality, that which minimizes the differences between the reported book value of the asset and its market value over the life of the asset.

HOW TO ALLOCATE AND VALUE THE INVENTORY

Another important decision for many businesses is how to handle inventory costs. These costs are enormous for many businesses, especially those that have large manufacturing, wholesale, or retail trade operations. How those costs are accounted for can have a major impact on the company's income taxes and, hence, on its bottom line.

The physical inventory of a business can show up on its financial statements in two distinct parts: one part allocated as the asset inventory, and the other part showing up as having been directly associated with revenues, under cost of goods sold (COGS) on the income statement (a reduction in inventory on the balance sheet). For management purposes it is useful to identify specifically those units of inventory that have been sold to customers, since doing so tends to give a more accurate picture of the financial condition of the business; however, the cost of maintaining such a level of accounting detail can't always be justified by the value of doing so.

The allocation of physical inventory between the asset inventory and the expense COGS will depend on how the business selects among three sets of accounting conventions:

Whether it chooses the *periodic* or the *perpetual* inventory method. Under the periodic inventory method, the expense COGS is calculated as the beginning inventory plus purchases minus the ending inventory; under the perpetual inventory method, the asset inventory is calculated as the beginning inventory plus purchases minus withdrawals. The periodic method is generally preferable when the inventory consists of a large volume of inexpensive items; the perpetual method tends to be more suitable when the cost of running out of merchandise is large.

Whether it values its inventory on the basis of *historical* (or *acquisition*) cost, *current* cost, or the *lower-of-cost-or-market* cost basis.

Whether it values the units in the ending inventory on the basis of the cost of the oldest items in the inventory (the *first-in, first-out*, or FIFO method), the cost of the most recent items (the *last-in, first-out* or LIFO method), or the weighted average of all the items (the *weighted average* method). When the prices of the goods in the inventory rise, LIFO produces a higher COGS number, thus reducing pretax profit, income taxes, and aftertax profit; FIFO, on the other hand, presents a more realistic picture of the current worth of the inventory.

The selection among the last of the three sets of options noted above—whether to use the FIFO, LIFO, or weighted average method of treating inventory cost flow—presents the exception to the rule that different generally accepted accounting principles can be used for tax and financial reporting purposes. The business can't, for example, use LIFO for tax purposes and FIFO for financial reporting purposes.

ACCOUNTING CONVENTIONS THAT REDUCE TAXES: A SUMMARY OF ESSENTIAL PRINCIPLES

Within the realm of generally acceptable accounting principles, a variety of options are available to the firm. The selections among those options can have profound effects on the firm's taxes for a given period. The firm can influence how much income taxes it can avoid or defer to a later period in its selection of:

The form of its business organization—whether a corporation, a partnership, a corporation taxed as a partnership, an S corporation, or a proprietorship;

The degree to which it finances its assets with debt rather than equity (since interest payments on debt are tax deductible, while dividend payments to equity owners are not);

The month it uses to end its fiscal year;

When it reports revenues and expenses—that is, whether it uses the accrual or cash method of accounting;

The method it uses to depreciate its long-term assets—whether it uses the straight-line depreciation method or one of the accelerated methods (double declining balance method, sum-of-the-years'-digits method, or accelerated cost recovery system [ACRS]); and

How it allocates and values its inventory—whether it chooses the periodic or the perpetual inventory method; whether it values its inventory on the basis of historical costs, current costs, or the lower-of-cost-or-market cost basis; and whether it values its inventory cost flows using the FIFO, LIFO, or weighted average method.

In selecting among these alternatives, tax avoidance (not to be confused with tax evasion, the willful and fraudulent concealment of a taxpayer's tax liability from the Internal Revenue Service) is a perfectly legal and prudent consideration. Most companies count on good tax lawyers or tax accountants—large companies use both—to provide guidance on how to report. The right choices can significantly improve the firm's bottom line.

4

THE INCOME STATEMENT AS A TOOL FOR MANAGING OPERATIONS

In business the earning of profit is something more than an incident of success. It is an essential condition of success; because the continued absence of profit itself spells failure.

—JUSTICE LOUIS D. BRANDEIS

The income statement provides the familiar bottom line of the business—net profit. Thus, it serves as the official scorecard of a business, a certificate of its viability as a profitable enterprise. It also summarizes the essential ingredients of the bottom line: revenues, cost of goods sold, and operating expenses.

The income statement is capable, however, of providing much more. With a properly structured set of accounts, the income statement can give managers information that is consistently richer, more tangible, more relevant, and hence more useful about the operations of the business than information available from any other source. The income statement is capable of revealing to management not only information about how the business is doing as a whole, but about how each *piece* of the business is doing—each profit center or business segment.

THE BASIC STRUCTURE OF THE INCOME STATEMENT

To see how the income statement can do all this, let's begin with the fundamentals. The income statement provides information about the performance of a business over a particular period of time. It provides details about the formula:

$$\text{Net income} = \text{Revenues} - \text{Costs}.$$

It does so, first, by partitioning costs into those that are immediately related to revenues and those that are not.

For a business that sells products, the costs that are immediately related to revenues are the costs of manufacturing or purchasing those products. Those costs are called the *cost of goods sold* (COGS). For a business that sells services, the costs that are directly associated with revenues, usually labor costs, are called the *cost of sales* (COS).

The costs that the business incurs pretty much regardless of the volume of its revenues are called its *operating expenses*. Operating expenses consist typically of *selling expenses* (e.g., salespersons' salaries and commissions, their fringe benefits and travel costs, advertising, depreciation of store equipment, and marketing overhead costs) and *administrative expenses* (e.g., officers' salaries, rent, utilities, depreciation of office equipment, and accounting and legal costs). Another expense that is largely unrelated to a company's revenues level is *research and development expense*.

(Note that expenses are not always the same as cash outlays. Depreciation and amortization of assets, write-offs and write-downs for bad debts, and write-offs for inventory spoilage or obsolescence, are examples of expenses on the income statement that do not involve cash expenditures. Such differences between expenses and cash outlays contribute to the fact that

EXHIBIT 4-1
The Basic Structure of the Income Statement

Revenues	$1,000,000
(−) Cost of Goods Sold	600,000
(=) Gross Profit	400,000
(−) Operating Expenses	300,000
(=) Pretax Profit	100,000
(−) Income Taxes	20,000
(=) Net Profit	$ 80,000

income is often a weak determinant of the business's cash position. This issue is discussed further in Chapter 7.)

The allocation of costs between ones that are immediately related to the level of revenues (cost of goods sold) and ones that are indirectly related (operating expenses) is not an arbitrary one. Profitability *means* that the spread between revenues and the cost of goods sold (the spread is called *gross profit*) exceeds operating expenses. The business can be more profitable by increasing its sales by more than its cost of goods sold, or by decreasing its operating expenses, or both. It is useful to be able to understand the profitability of the business both in terms of its ability to increase its gross profit and in terms of its ability to control operating expenses. The income statement provides this useful view of the operations of the business.

The basic structure of the income statement is shown in Exhibit 4-1.

THE ANATOMY OF PROFIT

The business shown in Exhibit 4-1 made $80,000 of aftertax profit during the period. It did so, first, by selling $1 million of products and services. It did so, second, by keeping its cost of goods sold down to 60 percent of revenues, yielding $400,000 of gross profit. Third, it held operating costs down to 30 percent of revenues, leaving $100,000 of pretax profit. Fourth, it paid only $20,000 in income taxes, two percent of revenues, leaving $80,000 for reinvestment or distribution to the owners of the business.

Could the business have done better? Sure—by increasing its revenues, increasing its gross margin percentage (i.e., decreasing cost of goods sold as a percentage of revenues), lowering its operating expenses, or by lowering or deferring its income taxes.

(With respect to the second method of increasing profit, we will, henceforth, refer to increasing the *gross margin percentage* [i.e., gross profit as a percent of revenues] rather than decreasing cost of goods sold as a percent of revenues. While the two are equivalent, the former focuses on increasing the *spread* between revenues and the cost of goods sold, which is a more useful concept. It really is all right for the cost of goods sold to increase, as long as revenues increase by more.)

The four primary ways that a business can create or increase its profit are worth repeating:

Increase revenues

Increase gross profit as a percent of revenues

Decrease operating expenses as a percent of revenues

Decrease or defer income taxes as a percent of revenues.

In most businesses, it is possible to employ each of these four profit-growing strategies. Increasing revenues means more effective *marketing* (not just selling, but advertising, pricing, packaging, and positioning of products and services as well). Increasing the gross margin percentage means smarter purchasing. Decreasing operating expenses as a percent of revenues means tighter controls. And decreasing income taxes as a percent of revenues, or deferring income taxes, means smarter tax accounting (recall the principles discussed in Chapter 3).

A REAL-WORLD ILLUSTRATION

These four strategies can be examined more carefully if we turn from our hypothetical company to a real one. Take the International Business Machines Corporation, for example. Exhibit 4-2 displays for that corporation the same kind of information as was shown for our fictitious company in Exhibit 4-1.

Note, first, that IBM made $6.6 billion in aftertax profit in 1985. The numbers in this exhibit reflect not only a real business, but one that was large and extremely profitable as well. Indeed, in 1985, IBM was the most profitable corporation in the world. (It was dominant too, capturing 72 percent of the profit earned by the entire computing machinery industry in that year.)

Note, second, that two lines have been added to the income statement shown in Exhibit 4-1: Income from Operations and

EXHIBIT 4-2
Income Statement
International Business Machines Corporation
For the year ending December 31, 1985
(Billions)

Revenues	$50.1
(−) Cost of Goods & Services	21.1
(=) Gross Profit	29.0
(−) Operating Expenses	17.7
(=) Income from Operations	11.3
(−) Net Nonoperating Income	0.4
(=) Pretax Profit	11.6
(−) Income Taxes	5.1
(=) Net Profit	$ 6.6

Net Nonoperating Income. Those two lines are needed because IBM, like most large companies, pays interest and earns interest on money that it owes and is owed. Since interest paid and earned are not the immediate result of IBM's primary operations—the sale of business machines and related products and services—they show up on the income statement as Net Nonoperating Income (Net refers to the difference between IBM's 1985 nonoperating income of $832 million and its interest expense of $443 million).

The third, and most important, note is this: IBM's $6.6 billion bottom line is only the bottom line. The crucial, and more interesting, question is *how* IBM managed to make over $6 billion. It did so primarily in four ways:

$50 billion in revenues

gross profit 58 percent of revenues

operating expenses 35 percent of revenues

income taxes 10 percent of revenues.

These four measures, readily derived from IBM's 1985 income statement, reflect in a nutshell the facts that are most basic to IBM's profitability: (1) IBM has been an extremely effective marketing organization, yielding very high revenues; (2) it has purchased competitively and, because of its considerable goodwill, has been able to price its products and services toward the high end of the market, yielding both a high profit margin and a large sales volume; (3) it has controlled its operating costs effectively; and (4) while it has contributed enormously to government revenues, it has effectively deferred its income tax payments.

Exhibit 4-3 displays the four crucial components of profit for IBM in 1985 against comparable numbers for the same company in 1980.

Thus, IBM performed very well in 1980, and did still better in 1985 (even after adjusting for inflation, which is not shown

EXHIBIT 4-3
The Four Key Components of Profitability
IBM Corporation: 5-year Changes, 1980 to 1985

	1980	1985	% Change
Revenues (billions)	$26.2	$50.1	+91
Gross Profit % of Revenues	61.3%	57.5%	−6
Operating Expenses % of Revenues	39.4%	35.3%	−10
Income Taxes % of Revenues	8.9%	10.2%	+15
After-Tax Profit (billions)	$ 3.6	$ 6.6	+68

here). Its more than two-thirds increase in aftertax profit during that five-year period was primarily the result of a near doubling of its revenues, and secondarily the result of effective controls over the growth of its operating expenses. The increase in revenue alone easily offset a six percent decline in gross profit as a percent of revenues: Gross profit increased by $13 billion from 1980 to 1985.

So, IBM grew its profit during this period primarily by increasing its revenues by considerably more than its cost of goods sold and by controlling the growth of its operating costs. That sounds a little like motherhood-and-apple-pie, but it isn't. Some income statements reveal profits that result exclusively from a growth in gross profit; others reveal profits that result only from a reduction in operating costs. IBM was able to accomplish both, mostly the former. Many of IBM's competitors were unable to accomplish either. Big Blue didn't do quite as well in 1986, but that's another story, one that will be discussed later.

IMPROVING PROFITABILITY
BY BUSINESS SEGMENT

Thus, we can derive some important basic information about IBM's profit from its income statement. But we still don't know a whole lot about *how* IBM was able to expand its gross profits so substantially from 1980 to 1985. We'd like to know, specifically: In which parts of its business was IBM able to produce the greatest increases in gross profits? And which operating expenses was it most effectively able to control?

The basic idea here is essentially the same as that embodied in the 16th century maxim, *Separa et impera*—divide and conquer—except without the heavy-handed connotations that the maxim's author, Niccolo Machiavelli, intended. We can better understand the business by dividing it into its parts. And the income statement can help us to attain that understanding.

Which brings us back to a very important point made at the beginning of this chapter: The income statement is capable of revealing information not only about how the business as a whole is doing, but also about how each piece of the business is doing. This capability cannot be achieved, however, unless the business's accounting data are maintained in sufficient detail to give an accurate picture of how well each segment of the business is doing.

As with most well-managed companies, IBM maintains such data. Following generally accepted accounting principles, they provide the general public with an informative overview of how each gross component of their business—sales, services, and rentals—is performing. Such information is shown in Exhibit 4-4.

While not very detailed about business segments, Exhibit 4-4 does provide some basic information about how profitable each major category of IBM's business was in 1985. It reveals that over two-thirds of IBM's gross profit is attributable to sales. The comany's primary business, after all, is selling computers and related hardware and software. When compared with similar data from earlier years, IBM's income statement indicates also that rentals, while having a slightly higher gross profit margin than the other two gross categories of business, has declined in revenues by more than half during the period 1982 through

EXHIBIT 4-4
Gross Profit by Business Category
IBM Corporation—Year ending December 31, 1985
(Dollars in billions)

Business Category	Revenues	Cost of Goods Sold	Gross Profit	Gross Margin %
Sales	$34.4	$14.9	$19.5	57
Services	11.5	4.7	6.8	59
Rentals	4.1	1.5	2.6	64
Totals	$50.1	$21.1	$29.0	58

1985. IBM obviously does not envision a significant future in the computer rental market.

Further details about each major segment of IBM's operations—processors (i.e., computers), peripherals, office systems and workstations, program products (i.e., software), maintenance services, and others—are shown in Exhibit 4-5.

The information in Exhibit 4-5 provides details about *gross* income by segment, not *net* income by segment, so it really doesn't reveal the extent to which each type of IBM's business contributed to the company's $6.6 billion profit in 1985.

It provides some extremely useful information nonetheless.

EXHIBIT 4-5
Gross Income by Business Segment
IBM Corporation—Years ending December 31, 1983-85
(Dollars in billions)

Business Segment	1983	1984	1985	2-Year Increase
Processors	$10.7	$11.9	$12.1	$1.5
Peripherals	11.1	11.7	12.7	1.5
Office Systems	7.9	10.0	10.5	2.6
Program Products	2.3	3.2	4.2	1.9
Maintenance Svcs	4.6	5.3	6.1	1.5
All Other	3.6	3.9	4.4	0.8
Totals	$40.2	$45.9	$50.1	$9.9

Mostly, it reveals that IBM's business is changing significantly. The two largest components of the company's business, computers and peripherals, have not been the largest growth segments of the company's operations. The growth in IBM's office systems and workstations segment and in its software segment have been significantly larger, both absolutely and in percentage terms. Those two segments represented 25 percent of IBM's business in 1983 and 29 percent in 1985, while the computers and peripherals segments, collectively, declined from 54 percent to just under 50 percent of IBM's revenues. For a company as large and stable as IBM, such changes in the business mix don't normally occur over such a short time span.

CONTROLLING INDIRECT COSTS

What about IBM's control of the growth of its operating costs? IBM's public income statement shows two components of costs that are not directly to revenues: Selling and General and Administrative (G&A) Expenses, and Research, Development, and Engineering Expenses. The 5-year growth in each of those components is shown in Exhibit 4-6.

The growth in IBM's operating costs, as a whole, 72 percent, was less than the growth of IBM's gross profits, 80 percent, which is what profit-making is all about.

The two components, examined separately, however, reveal another important kernel of wisdom about IBM's success: IBM was more conscientious about controlling the growth of overhead-type costs (up 63 percent) during this period than it was about controlling the growth of its research and development costs (up 101 percent).

We will see in Chapter 11 that IBM's commitment to R&D spending is not as aggressive as some of its competitors in the computer industry. Big Blue has a reputation for conserva-

EXHIBIT 4-6
Change in Indirect Expenses
IBM Corporation—1980 to 1985
(Dollars in billions)

	1980	1985	Change*
Selling, G&A expenses	$ 8.0	$13.0	63%
R&D, engineering expenses	2.4	4.7	101%
Total	$10.3	$17.7	72%

*Columns 1 and 2 are rounded numbers; the changes shown are based on the more precise unrounded numbers.

tivism in research and development—allowing smaller, more enterprising companies to discover and develop new technologies. At the same time, however, IBM's $4.7 billion in R&D costs in 1985 is, by any measure, a huge commitment to R&D. That those expenses more than doubled during the five years shown indicates that the commitment has grown.

Of course, the level of detail about gross profits and indirect costs reported in the performance-by-segment part of IBM's annual reports is really insufficient for the corporation's mid-level managers. Processors, peripherals, office systems, software, and maintenance services are each multibillion-dollar business aggregates. IBM's corporate structure is in fact far more complex than that, and certainly more complex than sales, services, and rentals. In 1985, the company was organized, first, into a number of groups, with each group focusing on broad market areas or corporate functions (e.g., large computers and advanced technology; midsize computers and peripheral equipment; communications and personal computers; marketing); each group in turn consisted of two to four divisions. Even as it changes its organization chart, IBM maintains financial details for each group and division, and does so further by industry segment and class of product or service, such as those shown in Exhibit 4-4, and even by major client category (e.g., it has a Federal Systems Division). The company also maintains financial performance data by geographic area and by subsidiary. Detail about sales, service, and rentals is maintained within each of those business entities, and is further broken down by specific product line. This allows IBM to provide fairly detailed financial performance data to a large variety of profit centers among its corps of mid- and upper-level managers.

Full financial data for each of those smaller corporate entities do not appear in IBM's annual report, but the company does, nonetheless, rely on such data to gauge the performance of those entities. Thus IBM partitions its financial performance data not only into individual product and service lines that are substantially more detailed than is shown in the financial statements that appear in their annual reports, but also into specific corporate entities that are divided functionally and regionally.

HOW THE INCOME STATEMENT CAN SUPPORT BUSINESS DECISIONS

IBM, and most other successful companies, use this kind of information to expand, contract, or modify individual segments—profit and cost centers—of their operations. If a particular product of service line, functional division, regional operation or territory, subsidiary or other identifiable profit center shows chronically substandard performance, it is likely to be modified or discontinued. If the segment shows conspicuously strong financial performance, it is likely to be expanded, except when a prior strategic decision had been made to discontinue all but the most highly profitable aspects of the segment's operations, as in the case of IBM's rentals business. Managers who consistently surpass the performance norms for their segments of the firm's operation usually receive larger incentive bonuses than other managers. They tend also to be promoted to positions of higher responsibility more quickly.

Other factors that don't appear on the income statement must, of course, play an important role: internal corporate relations, enhancement of the company's goodwill, contribution to technological breakthroughs, and so on. Management can nonetheless realize improvement of its bottom line by promoting more of what contributes to the bottom line and less of what diminishes it.

In using financial performance data in this way, businesses must be especially careful about how they allocate costs and revenues. Marketing costs that show up on the financial statements of one segment, for example, may in fact support the revenues of another segment. Decisions to contract, expand, or otherwise modify any particular business segment should be cognizant of such slippages between actual performance of the segment and the performance that is reflected in its financial statements.

Operating costs can be similarly controlled. By breaking down operating costs in more detail, the business can better control those costs, in much the same way that it can increase gross profits by generating financial performance data by detailed operating segments of the business. When the business grows, this means examining the growth of each major component of operating expenses—selling costs, rent, utilities, administrative staff salaries, accounting and legal costs, and so on—to see that no particular component is growing out of hand. Each component of indirect cost might be controlled, for example, to grow at a slower rate than gross profit. Any especially large growth in an operating expense category or account should be justifiable in terms of its specific contribution to profit. When gross profit declines, the business should attempt to reduce each operating expense category, examining those components that can be reduced the most without jeopardizing future business.

The key to controlling operations and costs in this manner is accountability. To the extent that the financial data can, without great difficulty or expense, be modified to correspond more closely to actual operations, such data modifications should be made, so that managers can be held more closely accountable for both their successes and failures. To the extent that such modifications are impossible or impractical, the financial statements become less valuable as instruments of corporate policy, decision-making, and progress.

Most of us have known people who don't care to be held so closely accountable to financial performance measures. They are often inclined to attend more to the shortcomings of financial statements for performance assessment than to ways that they can improve their profitability numbers. Most experienced, competent managers, however, prefer to be held accountable for their bottom-line performance.

As long as the financial statements of the business have been made to correspond closely to the actual operations of each business segment, good managers can feel comfortable using those statements for essential decision making: expanding the more profitable lines of business and eliminating or selling off the less profitable ones; sometimes through merger with or acquisition of another firm; rewarding or promoting consistently profit-producing managers, and supporting others to do better; creating greater incentive for the sales staff to target on profits rather than sales, perhaps by augmenting or replacing commissions based on revenues with commissions based on the profits associated with their sales; and modifying advertising strategies for less successful product or service lines.

Thus the income statement can be an indispensable tool not only for reporting about the busines's profitability, but for improving it as well.

THE INCOME STATEMENT AS A TOOL FOR PROFITABILITY: ESSENTIALS

The income statement provides the fabled bottom line of the firm's success—profit—but it can provide much more. By organizing the financial data of the business by segment of the firm's operations—revenue and cost data for each profit center and cost data for each cost center—the firm's executives can induce an accountability for profits throughout the firm that effectively promotes more of what contributes to aggregate profit while reducing or eliminating what diminishes it.

Once the income statement data are organized by profit and cost center, the firm's managers can improve their awareness of profitability, and thus enhance it, by monitoring changes from one period to the next in four key dimensions of the statement:

Revenues

Gross profit as a percent of revenues

Operating expenses as a percent of revenues, and

Income taxes as a percent of revenues

The firm improves its profitability by increasing revenues (through more effective marketing in each profit center) and gross profit as a percent of revenues (through more effective purchasing), by controlling operating expenses as a percent of revenues (by reducing costs that do not contribute to profits in either the short or long term), and by decreasing or deferring income taxes as a percent of revenues (through the use of effective tax avoidance and deferral strategies).

Most profitable firms induce their managers to improve the performance of each profit and cost center through incentive bonuses and promotions for achieving or surpassing profit or cost control targets. Firms that are consistently profitable usually ensure that those incentive systems do not sacrifice long-term profits for profits in the near term—for example, by offering incentive pay not only for profits in the current period, but for meeting profit growth targets as well.

If you're serious about long-term growth, give your managers incentives to have *each and every* quarter's profits larger than those of the previous quarter. In the long run, corporations tend to wind up wherever their managers are induced to take them.

5

THE BALANCE SHEET AS A TOOL FOR MANAGING ASSETS AND FINANCES

Did you hear the one about the accountant who was asked, "What color is that horse over there?" He answered, "On this side it's brown."

—Anonymous

If the income statement answers the question, "How is our business doing?" the balance sheet answers the question, "Where does it stand?" The balance sheet does this by focusing both on what the business owns—its assets—and on how it has financed what it owns by means of debt and equity.

Like Net Income on the income statement, the balance sheet has its bottom line, too: Net Worth. Net worth is the business owners' equity: what is left over after the total debts owed by the business are subtracted from the total assets owned by the business. The balance in the balance sheet, in fact, represents a restatement of that definition of net worth:

$$\text{Assets} = \text{Liabilities} + \text{Equity}.$$

Thus assets, on the left or top part of the balance sheet, are in balance with the sum of liabilities plus capital, on the right or bottom part.

As was noted in Chapter 2, net worth, on the balance sheet, is closely related to the bottom line of the income statement: The net worth of the business at the end of any accounting period (usually a month, quarter, or year) is equal to the net worth at the start of that period plus the net income, or minus the net loss, that accumulated during the period.

Like the income statement, the balance sheet is used routinely to provide financial information for banks, prospective investors, and others outside the business. It normally provides details about the assets, liabilities, and equity of the company for those interested in getting a sense of what it's worth.

And like the income statement, the balance sheet offers the potential for considerably more essential information for management purposes. That potential has not been fully appreciated by most users of financial statements.

The practical power of the balance sheet as a tool for managing the business becomes especially apparent when successive periods are compared. Focusing on changes in the balance sheet can direct management's attention to the uses to which profits have been put, and can be put, and the manner in which losses have been or might be financed. It can inform the manager specifically about expansion, diversification, financing options, and risk. And it can provide critical information about management's adherence to its plan for improved or sustained profitability. These balance sheet uses will become clearer after a discussion of a few fundamentals.

THE BASIC STRUCTURE OF THE BALANCE SHEET

The balance sheet is divided in two ways. First, it is divided in terms of *assets* (the left-hand side) versus *liabilities* and *owners' equity* (the right-hand side). Second, it is divided in terms of the *short term* (up to one year) and the *long term* (more than a year): Both assets and liabilities are divided into short- (current)

EXHIBIT 5-1
The Basic Structure of the Balance Sheet

Assets	Liabilities
Current Assets:	*Current Liabilities:*
Cash	Accounts Payable
Marketable Securities	Current Part of Long-
Accounts Receivable	Term Liabilities
Inventory	Client Deposits
Fixed Assets:	*Long-Term Liabilities:*
Property and Equipment	Notes Payable
Investments	Mortgages Payable
Goodwill	Contracts Payable
	Owners' Equity
	Contributed Capital
	Retained Earnings

and long-term elements. Those elements are shown in Exhibit 5-1.

The assets and liabilities are usually sorted on the balance sheet approximately by the average life of the items in each category of asset or liability. Current assets and current liabilities—assets and liabilities that are expected to be converted to cash transactions within one year—appear before fixed assets and long-term liabilities. Among the current assets, the cash and marketable security items are the most liquid of the assets of the business, so they generally appear first.

What, precisely, are assets? The *assets* of the business are its resources, the things that give it the ability to generate profits. Assets are generally convertible into money. Most assets are tangible, such as cash, supplies, inventory, furniture, and machinery, but for some businesses the most valuable assets are intangible. The values of all the assets shown on the formal balance sheet are book values: purchase cost less accumulated write-offs, such as depreciation.

Notice that one of the fixed assets shown in Exhibit 5-1 is the intangible asset, Goodwill. Goodwill appears as an asset on the

formal balance sheet only when the business has been purchased previously for an amount that exceeds the total book
value of its assets. Goodwill is the amount of that excess. (Some
companies have negative goodwill.) Because market values
change, the amount of goodwill on the balance sheet is not
generally an up-to-date reflection of the actual difference between the company's market value and the book value of its
assets—more will be said about that in a later section of this
chapter. When it does appear on the balance sheet, goodwill
is amortized as a fixed asset over a period of up to 40 years;
hence, it declines in value on the balance sheet even when the
actual market value of the business may be increasing. We will
take a closer look at goodwill and other intangible assets later in
this chapter.

Liabilities are the debts of the business. They represent the
accumulation of the firm's past and present financial obligations to provide goods and services, obligations that require
settlement. The business accumulates liabilities by incurring
expenses, recognizing losses, and by receiving assets.

The *owners' equity* is the amount that remains after the liabilities are subtracted from the assets. Owners' equity consists of
two parts: the amount that has been provided by the owners of
the business (Contributed Capital), and the amount that has
been generated by the business in the form of profits (Retained
Earnings). When the business is organized as a corporation,
the contributed capital consists of shares of stock.

THE BALANCE SHEET PROBLEM: REPORTED AMOUNTS DO NOT ALWAYS REFLECT CURRENT MARKET REALITY

The balance sheet is often considered less useful for management purposes than the income statement because the values
reported on it are not generally the same as current market

values. The book values shown on the formal balance sheet do, in fact, frequently depart from current market values. Why? To begin with, the business may have purchased its assets at prices that were, at the time of purchase, either below or above the prevailing market prices. Then, over time, the market values of the business's various assets change in relation to the prices of other goods and services, some more than others. This happens because the tastes of customers usually change, new technologies render different assets obsolete at different rates, inventories sometimes spoil, competition often intensifies, and so on.

Over a period of time, the book values of the assets of the business tend to depart from the market values for another basic reason: general inflation of the dollar. Book values are not adjusted for inflation, and inflation causes the market prices of most goods to increase. This tends to be the case especially for real estate owned by the business. Real property doesn't generally spoil or grow obsolete, so it's not depreciated; but inflation alone usually causes the market value of this asset to increase, while the book value of the property stays constant on the balance sheet. For most other assets, inflation tends to soften the effect of obsolescence, but rarely offsets it.

Obsolescence and other factors that tend to depress the market values of assets can, of course, be explicitly accounted for. Current assets that decline in value due to unforeseen circumstances can be adjusted downward through the taking of write-offs and the creation of reserve accounts. For example, accounts receivable that eventually become uncollectable can be written down before it is known which specific accounts will fall into that category by creating the contra account, Reserve for Bad Debts, and applying an historically valid bad debt percentage against the firm's entire pool of accounts receivable. Inventory spoilage can be accounted for explicitly by taking a write-off when the spoilage is realized, or a write-down when it is predictable. And fixed assets are adjusted downward through depreciation.

Adjusting asset values downward for such purposes does not, however, always bring book values into close alignment with market values. For example, the adjustment for uncollectable accounts receivable, Reserve for Bad Debts, may have been overly pessimistic, in which case the accounts receivable shown on the balance sheet would understate their actual market worth. And in depreciating a fixed asset, the assumed life of the asset and the depreciation method used by the business to diminish the book value of the asset often end up providing a poor approximation of the actual rate at which the asset wears out, grows obsolete, or becomes unpopular, and thus declines in value. Surely, many billions of dollars worth of currently used assets that are highly productive have been fully depreciated by the businesses that use them.

ANOTHER BALANCE SHEET DISTORTION: INTANGIBLE ASSETS

The company's formal balance sheet is often a poor reflection of the market worth of the company for yet another reason: Its *intangible assets* may bear little resemblance to reality, or they may not be reported at all.

Not all of the assets of the business can be seen and touched. For many companies the most valuable asset, goodwill, is absent from the balance sheet altogether. Remember, goodwill appears on the balance sheet only when the business has previously been sold. Even for those companies, the amount shown on the balance sheet tends to depart from the market value of goodwill as the years pass—sometimes overstating it and sometimes understating it.

How does a company generate goodwill? By selling high-quality goods and services, advertising them effectively, pricing them competitively, and maintaining excellent relations with the customers. This usually means hiring and training competent personnel and managing them well. It can also mean establishing and maintaining favorable sources of capital and loans, good relations with vendors, and effective legal and financial counsel. And selecting an advantageous location in the first place.

Other intangible assets whose book values often depart from market values can show up on the balance sheet, when a financial transaction has been made involving such assets. *Patents* are one such example. They give the business an exclusive, 17-year right to use a specific process or make a specific product. *Copyrights* are another. They give the business an exclusive, 28-year right to a specific written work or art object. *Trademarks*, another intangible asset, give the business the exclusive and continuing right to use specific names or symbols to identify a brand or family of products. *Franchises* represent yet another type of intangible asset, which gives exclusive rights to a business to operate or sell a specific line of products or services in a particular geographical area.

Patents, copyrights, trademarks, and franchises, when they appear on the balance sheet, appear as fixed assets at cost, less accumulated amortization. Patents and copyrights are amortized within 17 and 28 years, respectively; for trademarks and franchises, like goodwill, the amortization period may not exceed 40 years, even though the goodwill associated with those assets may outlive that time limit.

HOW MUCH DISTORTION?

The discrepancy between the book values and market values can be substantial. For publicly traded companies, it can be estimated pretty easily. To get the book value of the company's net worth, just look at the total capital that appears on the balance sheet. To get the market value of the same corporation's net worth, you multiply the number of common shares of stock outstanding by the market price per share. Since the owners of the stock in the company have revealed that they are not willing to part with their shares at that price, the company is obviously worth at least that much to them.

Let's look at an example of the discrepancy between the book value and market value of the net worth of the corporation. IBM, once again, serves as a good illustration—in this case because the discrepancy is substantial. Take a look, first, at IBM's balance sheet, shown in Exhibit 5-2.

This balance sheet tells us that the book value of IBM's net worth was $32 billion at the end of 1985. At the same time, 616 million shares of IBM common stock were outstanding, and the trade price of a share of that stock was $150. Since the holders of IBM stock revealed an unwillingness to part with their shares at that price, one could say that the owners of IBM valued the company at least as high as $92 billion (616 million shrares times $150 per share). So IBM's stockholders value their company a whole lot more than would appear justifiable by the numbers on the balance sheet. The market view of IBM's net worth was nearly triple its book value at the end of 1985!

Does that mean that IBM's book value is incorrect by a factor of three? Not at all. Price Waterhouse's auditors have validated the accuracy of the book value of net worth reported in IBM's annual report. Nor does it mean that IBM's stockholders are incorrect in their assessment of the worth of IBM.

What causes the factor-of-three difference is essentially this: IBM's balance sheet is based exclusively on IBM's financial *history*, and IBM's stockholders base their assessment of IBM's worth on their view of its *future profitability*. If the stockholders are correct in their assessment, IBM's largest asset is a fund of unreported goodwill that is at least twice as large as all its other assets combined. To the accountant, this goodwill is a speculative amount that does not belong on the balance sheet.

EXHIBIT 5-2
Balance Sheet
International Business Machines Corporation
As of December 31, 1985
(Billions)

ASSETS

Current Assets:		
Cash	$0.9	
Marketable Securities	4.7	
Notes & Accounts Receivable	9.8	
Other Accounts Receivable	0.8	
Inventories	8.6	
Other Current Assets	1.3	
		26.1
Fixed Assets:		
Rental Machines & Parts	4.6	
Less: Accumulated Depreciation	−2.8	
		1.8
Plant & Other Property	29.8	
Less: Accumulated Depreciation	−12.0	
	17.8	
Investments & Other Assets	6.9	
Total Assets		$52.6

LIABILITIES & STOCKHOLDERS' EQUITY

Current Liabilities:		
Taxes	$3.1	
Loans Payable	1.3	
Accounts Payable	1.8	
Compensation & Benefits	2.5	
Deferred Income	0.4	
Other Current Liabilities	2.4	
		11.4
Long-Term Liabilities:		
Long-Term Debt	4.0	
Deferred Income Taxes	3.7	
Other Liabilities	1.6	
		9.2
Stockholders' Equity:		
Capital Stock	6.3	
Retained Earnings	27.2	
Less: Misc. Adjustments	−1.5	
		32.0
Total Liabilities & Equity		$52.6

55

MANAGING ASSETS WITH THE BALANCE SHEET

If the balance sheet can report values that are so different from actual market values, can it be useful as a management tool? You bet it can, for two reasons. First, a large discrepancy between balance sheet values and corresponding market values, such as the one we just saw in the case of IBM, accumulates typically over many accounting periods. The discrepancy that occurs in a single accounting period is usually considerably smaller than that. From one accounting period to the next, any discrepancy between the net worth that shows up on the balance sheet and the market worth of the company will amount to the same degree of discrepancy in the net income reported on the income statement. Remember, the net income (or loss) for an accounting period is equivalent to the increase (or decrease) in net worth from the start to the end of the period. The balance sheet's usefulness as a management tool revolves largely around questions about whether the company's short-term change in its mix of assets is in accord with its longer term plans for profitability, and about how the company will finance its short-and medium-term needs. If the income statement can be useful for management purposes, despite the small discrepancies between book values and market values, so can the balance sheet.

Second, just as the business can create, for management purposes, special income statements that differ from the ones used for external purposes, the business can also create management-oriented versions of the balance sheet that differ from the formal balance sheet. Like the income statements that are used for management purposes, the management-oriented balance sheet need not comply with generally accepted accounting principles.

So the differences between balance sheet book values and corresponding market values do not have to limit the usefulness of balance sheets for management purposes.

What, then, does a management-oriented balance sheet look like, and what can it be used for? It looks essentially like a formal balance sheet, except that it reports amounts for more detailed segments of the business. Like the management-oriented income statement, the balance sheet can be disaggregated into units that are most relevant to the needs of the managers of each part of the business.

As noted earlier, the balance sheet can address two of those needs:

the uses of assets

the sources of financing.

We can once again turn to the real-world example of IBM to see how this works. From January 1, 1981, through December 31, 1985, IBM's equity grew by $16 billion, essentially the amount of aftertax profit earned by the company during that period. IBM's executives could have used this additional capital either to purchase more profit-generating assets or to reduce its liabilities, or both. What did they end up doing with the $16 billion of capital? The answer is shown in Exhibit 5-3: more income-producing assets.

From the start of 1981 to the end of 1985, IBM increased its assets by $26 billion, $10 billion more than its growth in equity. The company thus not only did not use its profits to reduce its liabilities, it nearly doubled its total liabilities during this period. Why? Because IBM's officers believed that the additional $10 billion of debt-financed assets would probably generate enough profit to cover the interest on that debt and still have a substantial amount left over as additional profit. They weren't wrong.

Exhibit 5-3 also tells a little about where IBM's officers were steering the company during the early 1980s. The category of assets that IBM increased more than any other during this period was nonrental fixed assets—the company expanded them

EXHIBIT 5-3
Change in Balance Sheets: IBM—1980 to 1985
(Billions)

ASSETS	1985		1980		Increase	
Current Assets						
Cash	$0.9		$0.3		$0.6	
Marketable Securities	4.7		1.8		2.9	
Notes & A/R—Trade	9.8		4.6		5.2	
Other Accounts Receivable	0.8		0.3		0.5	
Inventories	8.6		2.3		6.3	
Other Current Assets	1.3		0.6		0.7	
Total Current Assets		26.1		9.9		16.1
Fixed Assets:						
Rental Machines & Parts	1.8		8.4		−6.6	
Plant & Other Property	17.8		6.6		11.2	
Other Fixed Assets	6.9		1.8		5.1	
Total Fixed Assets		26.6		16.8		9.8
Total Assets		$52.6		$26.7		$25.9
LIABILITIES & EQUITY						
Current Liabilities:						
Taxes	3.1		2.4		0.7	
Loans Payable	1.3		0.6		0.7	
Accounts Payable	1.8		0.7		1.1	
Compens'n & Benefits	2.5		1.4		1.1	
Deferred Income	0.4		0.3		0.1	
Other Current Liabs	2.4		1.1		1.2	
Total Current Liabs		11.4		6.5		4.9
Long-Term Liabilities		9.2		3.7		5.5
Stockholders' Equity:						
Capital Stock	6.3		4.0		2.3	
Retained Earnings	27.2		12.5		14.7	
Equity Adjustments	−1.5		0.0		−1.5	
Total Equity		32.0		16.5		15.5
Total Liabs & Equity		$52.6		$26.7		$25.9

by $16 billion, to nearly triple the 1980 level. In expanding plant
and long-term equipment, rather than, say, paying more dividends to its stockholders or increasing marketable securities,
IBM continued during the first half of the 1980s to work toward

a profitable future by investing in itself. In also increasing its inventories by $6 billion (nearly a four-fold increase) and its receivables by over $5 billion (more than double), the company was at the same time concentrating on its current business. It was able to expand these three major categories of assets—nonrental fixed assets, inventories, and receivables—by more than the amount of its growth in retained earnings and debt primarily because it decreased another asset category—rental equipment—by nearly $7 billion. (Recall from Chapter 4 other evidence that IBM had chosen to reduce that line of business during this 5-year period.)

IBM's balance sheets thus provided its managers with critical periodic information about their success in carrying out their longer term plan for the growth of some lines of business and the contraction of others.

The balance sheet can provide much additional useful information when it is broken down in more detail for management purposes—when it is disaggregated for particular business segments, like the income statement. While IBM does not report balance sheet details by segment in its annual report to stockholders, it does maintain such reports for management purposes. By comparing such balance sheets from one point in time to another, the manager of a particular segment can establish whether the change in that segment's asset mix is consistent with the company's short-term and long-term plans for that segment.

MANAGING FINANCES WITH THE BALANCE SHEET

If the left-hand side of the balance sheet is useful for managing the firm's asset mix, the right-hand side is useful for managing its finances. The balance sheet can provide useful information both when the company wishes to raise funds needed to increase its assets and when it needs funds to cover its losses. Let's see how this works.

In terms of the balance sheet (in Chapter 7 we take a more comprehensive approach), the business can create new funds in any or all of three ways:

by raising additional capital

by increasing its liabilities

by reducing the levels of its less profitable assets.

In Exhibit 5-3 we saw how IBM financed its asset growth first by increasing equity by 94 percent; second, by increasing liabilities by 101 percent; and, third, by reducing rental equipment, a large and less desirable category of assets, by 78 percent. How are such percentages arrived at? Partly by plan and partly by circumstances that are difficult to control.

The officers of most successful companies today develop strategic plans that include elements of business development and asset growth and, often, elements of business segment contraction and an accompanying plan for liquidating or gradually retiring certain assets. Their skill in executing that plan and in selling it to the financial community will heavily govern their ability to achieve specific targets of growth and contraction. In addition, the company's officers usually have strong views about the extent to which they are willing to dilute their ownership control by bringing in outside capital, how much debt they are willing to incur at prevailing interest rates, and the extent to which they are willing to use their own assets, or those of the business, as collateral to secure loans. Those parts of financial management are controllable.

Less controllable are the specific decisions of prospective customers, actions of competing businesses, changes in the prices of goods and services needed by the business, movements in prevailing interest rates, changes in the availability of new capital, shifts in government policies and rulings that affect the general economy and the particular firm's market, and a host of other factors. Effectively managed companies can influence some of these factors, but usually end up having to modify their targets in response to them.

Financial management deals with both the factors that are under management's control and those that are more difficult to control. It begins with the strategic plan, discussed in more detail in Chapter 8. Strategic planning, according to Peter Drucker, arguably the world's leading authority on management,

is the continuous process of making present entrepreneurial (risk-taking) decisions systematically and with the greatest knowledge of their futurity; organizing systematically the efforts needed to carry out these decisions; and measuring the results of these decisions against the expectations through organized, systematic feedback.*

Strategic planning, in short, attempts to take the mystery out of the future of the business. It allows managers to shift events that govern financial success from the realm of the unknown to that of the predictable, and thus converts the uncontrollable into the controllable. In developing a thoughtful prognosis of consumer buying patterns, the competition, and other pertinent aspects of the future, management can better identify:

the lines of business that are most likely to succeed and fail,

the assets needed to develop the most potentially profitable lines of business, and

the financial alternatives available to raise the funds needed to support the acquisition of those assets.

The balance sheet displays both the current asset mix and the current mix of debt and capital. In much the same way that

*Peter F. Drucker, *Management: Tasks, Responsibilities, Practices* (New York: Harper and Row, 1973), p. 125.

managers can track the change in the business's asset mix to examine the degree to which the strategic plan is being adhered to, managers can also track the change in the mix of debt and capital to see whether the financial side of the strategic plan is being met.

The change in IBM's mix of debt and capital that shows up on the right-hand side of the company's balance sheets for the 5-year period ending at the close of 1985 exemplifies the usefulness of the balance sheet in financial management. The 101 percent increase in IBM's liabilities during that period was clearly within its ability to control—more so than the 94 percent increase in its equity, which was created primarily by its profits. The largest part of the increase in debt was long-term (a 147 percent increase), rather than current (75 percent increase). IBM fully controlled the extent to which it increased both its long-term debt (by issuing corporate bonds and obtaining notes from financial institutions), and most of its current debt; it was able to use its balance sheets to monitor the growth in those financial instruments. The increase in its total equity, on the other hand, was essentially equivalent to its net income during the period, which was not fully controllable. The degree to which each of those numbers, the fully controllable and not fully controllable, departed from IBM's plan is information that is closely held by the company.

Regardless of the precise degree of those departures from the plan, IBM's spectacular financial performance during the early 1980s makes it clear that the least painful way of raising funds is by generating profit. Raising capital other than retained earnings often means diluting the ownership of the business. Increasing debt means paying interest and, if the debt is not repaid on schedule, risking bankruptcy. Selling assets often means depriving the business of the future profits that those assets would otherwise generate. IBM's profit was the key that enabled it not to have to rely excessively on those more painful alternatives.

Its profit did not, however, enable it to ignore the determination of how much of each of those fund-raising alternatives to engage in. Profitable companies don't stay that way by becoming complacent. One standard way to determine how much of each approach to raising funds a business can afford, given the financial condition reflected in its current balance sheet, is by using financial ratio analysis, the subject of the next chapter.

When the balance sheet does reveal significant departures from a financial plan, such as when the business generates too little internal capital by falling short of its profit goals, it is important that management thoughtfully review its plan. It may be able to reverse a profit shortfall from one period to the next by keeping to the original plan. On the other hand, significant changes in the assumptions on which the plan was based may warrant a revision of the plan. We look deeper into the process of business planning in Chapter 8.

MANAGING WITH THE BALANCE SHEET: ESSENTIALS

The balance sheet provides basic information about the financial status of the business at a point in time—what assets the firm owns and how those assets are financed in terms of equity and debt. As the standard report card on the current financial health of the firm, the balance sheet indicates how much of an equity cushion the firm has—how financially able it is to expand or to sustain successive periods of losses without becoming insolvent.

Balance sheet numbers are subject to distortion because they represent book values, and book values tend to depart from market values increasingly over time for a variety of reasons. Some of those distortions can be reduced through the existence of sound procedures for depreciating long-term assets and adjusting values of short-term assets (e.g., a bad debt allowance for accounts receivable and a spoilage write-down for inventories), but intangible assets such as goodwill (resulting from advertising, a history of high quality service, etc.) and patents are either not reported at all (because no financial transaction involving them have occurred), or are reported at grossly distorted values.

The balance sheet is nonetheless valuable as a management tool because from one period to the next the differences in the reported values do not suffer from any more distortion than the income statement that corresponds to the same period. Like the income statement, the balance sheet can be useful for management purposes when it is structured and analyzed over time and by business segment. It can, in particular, permit an examination of the uses to which the firm puts its assets and the sources of the financing of those assets. When combined with information about the profit that results from the allocations of the firm's resources and the costs of financing those profits, the power of the balance sheet for managing becomes clear. We will look more closely at these issues in the next chapter and in Chapter 10.

6

USING FINANCIAL RATIOS TO IMPROVE THE BOTTOM LINE

Though pleased to see the dolphins play,
I mind my compass and my way

—MATTHEW GREEN

To know *that* the firm's profits have been positive or negative, large or small, is not to know *why*. In the last two chapters, we explored the most direct, and generally the most effective, way to learn why a company's bottom line is healthy or sick: break the financial statements down by business segment to see how well each component of the business is doing (each product and service line, department, branch, and so on). The profit whole, after all, is the sum of the profit parts.

Another way to diagnose the health of the business, and to do so fairly simply, is by calculating and monitoring financial ratios. *Financial ratio analysis* has, in fact, become the standard approach used by professional investors and lending institutions to quickly examine a company's financial statements so that the soundness of the company can be assessed based on a set of generally accepted standards. It is more than useful for the principals of the business to understand the fundamentals of financial ratio analysis, too, both to improve their communication with the financial community and to have additional tools available for their own understanding of how to use the financial statements as resources for the diagnosis and treatment of their company's well-being.

WHOSE BOTTOM LINE, REVISITED

Regardless of whether we analyze financial statements by segment or by using financial ratio analysis, we must first ask what the analysis is for, and for whom. Financial well-being isn't a concept that can be measured using a single metric that will be acceptable to all who are interested in the business.

Among prospective investors and lenders, the most widely accepted measure of the health of the business is the number at the bottom of the income statement. While not perfect, a company's demonstrated and sustained ability to produce profit is the clearest and most relevant single indicator available about the viability of the business.

Net profit is not, however, the most crucial concern of all who care about the financial performance of the business. Recall from Chapter 2 that the owners of the business may have a legitimate interest in drawing profits out of the business in the form of salaries, bonuses, or dividends rather than have them show up as business profits and be taxed accordingly; a stockholder is more likely to focus on dividends and capital gains, or on earnings per share (net profit divided by the number of shares outstanding); the chief financial officer can sometimes argue persuasively that cash flow is all that matters; a department or branch manager is more likely to watch his unit's operating profit as a percentage of the assets of the unit; and so on. Financial ratios can help to support each of those interests.

EFFECTIVENESS AND EFFICIENCY

Regardless of whose objectives we may wish to attend to, measuring the financial performance of the business or some aspect of it isn't fundamentally different from measuring the performance of anything else capable of performing—the economy, an athletic team or player, or an automobile, for instance. To assess performance, we can use measures of effectiveness or we can use efficiency measures or, better still, we can use both. *Effectiveness* measures have to do with output, productivity, or performance. The firm's net profit is such a measure. Similarly, the economy's effectiveness is often measured in terms of its gross national product or the number of jobs it creates; an athletic team's effectiveness is usually measured by how many more games it wins than it loses; and a racing vehicle's effectiveness is measured by its speed.

Efficiency measures have to do with effectiveness or output *per unit of input*. The firm's earnings per share and a division's operating per dollar of its assets are examples of efficiency measures. Notice that both of these measures are financial ratios. Similarly, the economy's efficiency is often measured in terms of productivity per worker; a player's efficiency is measured in terms of the number of successes (hits, baskets, etc.) per attempt (times at bat, shots taken); and a vehicle's fuel efficiency is usually measured in terms of the number of miles driven per gallon of gasoline consumed.

So efficiency measures are always ratios. Not all financial ratios are efficiency measures, however. Some financial ratios, as we'll see in a moment, measure how long it takes for a variety of important business events to occur—how long it takes for bills to get paid, for example, and for inventory to turn over.

PROFITABILITY RATIOS

The most basic financial ratios focus on the bottom line. For the owners of the business, a basic goal is to maximize the return on their investment. Let's look at how this goal, profitability, can be measured both for the corporation and for the partnership or proprietorship.

In a corporation, the owner is the stockholder, and for that individual the profitability ratio *return on investment* consists of the sum of dividends and capital gains (this sum is a measure of financial output), expressed as a percent of the initial investment (an input measure). If, for example, an investor buys $1000 worth of stock at the start of a year, earns $50 in dividends during the year, and then sells the stock at the end of the year for $1100, the pretax return on investment, ignoring brokers' fees and other transaction costs, would be 15 percent (the sum of $50 in dividends and $100 in capital gains as a percent of $1000).

Since the financial community can't easily keep track of the capital gains and dividend components of return on investment separately for each stockholder of a corporation, it uses instead the convention of measuring profitability based on more readily available corporate data. Two counterparts to the return-on-investment calculation for stockholders are earnings per share and return on stockholders' equity. *Earnings per share* is a standard, easy-to-calculate profitability ratio. It is simply the ratio of corporate aftertax profit (a measure of financial output for the corporation as a whole, rather than for the individual stockholder) to the number of shares of stock outstanding (the relevant input measure for the corporation as a whole). *Return on stockholders' equity* is the ratio of corporate profit to the average dollar value of corporate equity during the period, expressed as a percent.

In 1985, IBM's aftertax profit was $6.6 billion, and an average of 614 million shares of stock were outstanding during the year, so IBM earned nearly $11 of profit per share. The return on equity for IBM's stockholders (coporate profit as a percentage of the average stockholders' equity) was 22 percent.

For the proprietorship or partnership, the owner's equity is not held in the form of a stock certificate; return on investment is, nonetheless, a valid profitability measure for such enterprises. The return on investment calculation is usually less straightforward in this case, however, for two reasons: (1) the financial output measure typically includes both the profits of the business and the salary and nonsalary benefits to the proprietor or partner, and (2) the financial input measure includes both the capital investment and the market value of the time given to the business by the proprietor or partner as an employee. Since the principals in a small business have considerable latitude in determining their pay and benefits, it may not be especially useful to attempt to separate those benefits from their respective shares of the profits of the business.

Regardless of how the business is organized, it's useful to get beneath the return on investment numbers by examining some standard interim measures of profitability. Three such measures are the firm's gross profit margin, its operating profit margin, and its net profit margin. These are the most immediate measures of the firm's profitability; they come right off of the income statement.

The *gross profit margin* (or simply gross margin) is generally expressed as gross profit as a percentage of sales. It measures the rate at which each dollar of sales for a period contributes to gross profit for that period—the result of both the extent to which the firm first marked up each unit of good sold and then turned in a high sales volume on those goods. The higher the gross profit margin, the easier it is for the firm to cover its operating expenses. However, the higher the gross profit margin, the more attractive it is generally for the competition to take sales away from the firm and thus reduce sales volume. This trade-off is discussed more fully in Chapter 9, on pricing for profits. IBM's gross profit margin for 1985 was 58 percent ($29 billion in gross profit as a percent of its $50 billion in revenues).

The *operating profit margin* is generally calculated as operating profit (gross profit less operating expenses) as a percentage of sales. It measures the rate at which each dollar of sales contributes to operating profit. The *net profit margin* is like the operating profit margin, except that it includes nonoperating profit (interest income less interest expenses). It is usually expressed as net income as a percentage of sales. For IBM, the operating profit margin in 1985 was 22.6 percent, and the net profit margin was 23.2 percent.

LIQUIDITY (SHORT-TERM SOLVENCY) RATIOS

Profitability is by no means all that matters. The profitable business that is not conscious of how much cash is on hand to pay the bills can wind up in the same sorry position as the chronically unprofitable business. Profits usually can help a firm to alleviate a cash crunch, but only if the cash proceeds associated with those profits arrive in time to meet critical payables. Profitable companies that use their profits to finance rapid expansion can easily become insolvent in the short term if they do not carefully manage their cash receipts, payments, and new financial commitments. In the next chapter we'll examine in some detail how such cash crises can be avoided using procedures that are more thorough than those discussed here. In the meantime, we can look at a number of rough-and-ready financial ratios that are useful barometers for assessing the firm's short-term solvency—its ability to avert a cash crunch.

The most commonly used liquidity ratio is the *current ratio*—the ratio of current assets to current liabilities. Recall that current assets include cash and other assets that are converted to cash fairly quickly through normal operations, directly or indirectly, and current liabilities are debts to be paid soon. Technically, "current" means "within 12 months" in the accounting profession, but short-term solvency generally relates to the next few weeks or, when cash problems become really severe, the next few days (or even hours!). A business is usually vulnerable to a cash crisis when it has no working capital—that is, when its current liabilities equal or exceed its current assets. (Since *working capital* is defined as current assets minus current liabilities, the current ratio is sometimes called the working capital ratio.)

The current ratio is generally used by bankers and investors in sizing up a firm's solvency, but when combined with more detailed cash flow projections, it can also be an important tool for the firm's managers. Many firms try to maintain a current ratio in the neighborhood of two-to-one—they try to keep current assets about twice as large as current liabilities. The proper ratio for a particular firm will depend on the nature of the business, its access to financial resources, and a variety of other factors. (IBM's current ratio at the end of 1985 was 2.3-to-1.) When the current ratio falls into the danger zone—wherever that may be for any given business—that can be an important signal for the firm to make a detailed projection of cash and, perhaps, to begin to expand existing sources of financing or find new ones.

The current ratio is not the best indicator of liquidity for all businesses. For many businesses, the largest single component of current assets is inventory, and inventories can't always be converted to cash quickly enough to avert a cash disaster. For those firms, a better measure of liquidity is the *quick ratio* or *acid test ratio:* current assets other than inventory divided by current liabilities. A quick ratio of 1-to-1 is often regarded as sufficient, since that number means that cash, marketable securities, and current receivables match current liabilities (At the end of 1985 IBM's quick ratio was 1.5-to-1.)

Regardless of whether a firm uses the current ratio or the quick ratio, it is important that the ratio be treated primarily as a guidepost. These ratios are more useful for providing a rough sense of the firm's short-term solvency than for seriously managing the firm's cash position. Any particular value of either ratio can provide a misleading picture, since these ratios ignore a host of factors that can be extremely important: the composition of current assets and current liabilities, the timing of receivables and payables due, the seasonality of the business, and so on.

LIQUIDITY-RELATED RATIOS: RECEIVABLES, PAYABLES, AND INVENTORY

Because the timing of receivables and payables, and the size and nature of the inventory, can be critical to the short-term solvency of the firm, it is worthwhile for managers to make use of ratios that monitor those entities, too. The financial managers of cash-starved companies often end up having to focus primarily on receivables and payables, and occasionally find themselves having to liquidate inventory. At such times, the grim adage "collect early and pay late" can divert the attention of management from every other activity of the business.

The most common ratios for tracking receivables and payables measure the average length of time it takes to collect or pay the company's bills. The company's cash position is improved when the average time to collect accounts receivable is short, and when the average time to pay accounts payable is long.

For most companies, "collect early" can be an effective way to relieve a cash shortage. Accounts receivable are, as a rule, the company's most liquid asset after cash and marketable securities, and they are often a sizable asset as well. Many businesses are, in fact, quite lax about collecting accounts receivable. While an aggressive collection policy can cause loss of business, collections can generally be speeded up without such losses. Modest discounts for cash transactions can be an effective way to reduce chronically large receivables and increase cash. Interest charges for accounts that are at least 30 days old can be another. Customers whose accounts are 30 or 60 days past due generally expect well-managed businesses to send friendly reminders to pay their bills, and often expect to pay interest charges if they don't. Customers with accounts 90 days past due shouldn't be surprised to receive assertive—not rude—reminders to pay up. Many businesses do not routinely send notices at the 60- and 90-day points.

To monitor the collection of receivables, the manager can keep track of the average number of days it takes to collect accounts receivable. To do so, it's not necessary to calculate the age of each and every customer's debt and divide the total by the number of customers. A fairly accurate estimate of the *average collection period* in days can be obtained much more easily by dividing the average size of accounts receivable from successive balance sheets by the average daily revenues of the business. If, for example, a business starts the year with $50,000 in receivables and ends it with $70,000, then the average level of accounts receivable for the year can, for the sake of simplicity, be presumed to be $60,000. If, in addition, the firm's annual revenues were $730,000, or $2000 per day, the average dollar collected can be estimated to have taken 30 days to collect. (If the logic of this calculation isn't yet apparent, think of it in reverse: If revenues were $2000 per day, and it took 30 days to collect each dollar of revenue, then $60,000 of accounts receivable would accumulate by the time the customers paid their bills.)

Suppose, further, that the company's sales are distributed evenly throughout the calendar month and that the chief financial officer of the firm wanted to consider switching from a policy of billing all customers at the same time each month to one of billing them at the time of delivery. The average reduction in collection time would be half a month, or 15 days. Such a switch would reduce the firm's average receivables from $60,000 to $30,000—the equivalent of a $30,000 interest-free loan worth, say, $3000 of interest not paid. If the additional bookkeeping costs of such a policy change were to exceed $3000, then the old policy would be retained.

The other side of the coin is the company as a payer of the vendors' bills; in this case, "pay late" can be an effective way to increase cash, although often at the risk of jeopardizing relations with the vendors. The cost of late payments are sometimes explicit in the form of interest charges and discounts lost for failure to pay early.

Monitoring the payment of accounts payable is virtually the same as monitoring the receivables, except from the opposite point of view. The *average payables period* in days is estimated as the average accounts payable during the year divided by the daily cost of goods sold. (You can use the numbers in the receivables example, above, substituting payables for receivables and cost of sales for revenues, to see how this works.)

The firm's liquidity is also affected by its inventory. Cash is created when inventory is liquidated, or when the inventory turns over faster. (Why does faster inventory turnover mean more cash? Because the cost of goods sold is determined by the cost of the inventory at the average inventory level multiplied by the average number of times each inventory item has to be replaced during the year; for a given level of business, with a given cost-of-goods-sold level, the company can either increase the inventory level and allow the inventory to turn over more slowly or reduce the inventory and turn it over faster. Less inventory means more cash.) Turning the inventory over faster is generally a preferable way to generate cash because that approach does not usually diminish subsequent revenues to the extent that liquidation does. Some inventory items, of course, may be worth liquidating not just to raise needed cash, but because the inventory holding costs (space, maintenance, spoilage, and so on) are higher than the expected proceeds from the eventual sale of the inventory at current prices.

How can the inventory be turned over faster without a substantial increase in other costs (such as the cost of business lost due to inventory outages and the cost of more elaborate inventory management systems)? For most businesses, the cost of computerized inventory management systems is now sufficiently small to justify the use of such systems for tighter inventory control.

Inventory turnover can be measured using the *inventory turnover rate*, the ratio of cost of goods sold for the period to the average inventory during the period. This rate indicates whether the firm is tying up too much of its resources in the form of capital. It reflects, specifically, the number of times the typical item of inventory was sold and replaced by a new item during the period. If, for example, the inventory had a value of $8000 at the start of the year and $12,000 at the end of the year, then the average inventory value during the year can be roughly estimated to be $10,000. If, in addition, each item of inventory were held for an average of six months, then the cost of goods sold would be twice the average inventory; in that case, the cost of goods sold would be $20,000, and the inventory turnover rate would be $20,000/$10,000, or two times. The average inventory can be calculated directly from successive balance sheets, and the cost of goods sold is an income statement number, so the inventory turnover rate can be estimated readily from these two basic financial statements.

FINANCIAL LEVERAGE (LONG-TERM SOLVENCY) RATIOS

The third major group of financial ratios, no less important than the profitability and liquidity ratios, are the ratios of financial leverage. (If efficiency is a term from physics that can be usefully applied to the management of a business, so is leverage.) *Leverage* refers generally to the advantage associated with a device that produces more results than would otherwise be produced if the same amount of effort were applied in a more direct manner. Financial leverage refers specifically to the profit-generating potential of financial resources other than the firm's own capital.

Highly leveraged firms are able to create more profit-generating assets per dollar of capital than other firms because they rely more heavily on debt financing; rather than raise more capital, highly leveraged firms increase liabilities. If those additional debt-financed assets actually generate profits above and beyond the interest on the additional debt, the company will have produced its own capital, in the form of retained earnings, from the capital of others. There is a tax advantage to boot: When dividend-paying corporations increase leverage, they usually substitute interest costs, which are tax deductible, for dividend payments, which are not; the result is less taxes per dollar of pretax profit.

Leverage, however, is not a free lunch. A highly leveraged firm that is not able to create additional profits from the additional debt is left with higher interest costs than lower leveraged firms with the same amount of capital. If the firm incurs losses that are large relative to its cushion of equity, it risks bankruptcy. Not surprisingly, most creditors prefer to extend loans to companies that have a larger equity cushion, since the larger cushion reduces the likelihood of a default on the loan.

The most basic measure of the firm's financial leverage is its *debt-to-equity ratio*, simply the ratio of the firm's total liabilities to its total equity. (Some firms exclude current liabilities from the numerator of the ratio, under the notion that current liabilities are not really an alternative to capital as a way of raising profit-generating assets; either measure is acceptable for most businesses.) IBM's debt-to-equity ratio at the end of 1985 was 0.64-to-1; it raised an additional 64 cents worth of profit-producing assets from its various debt instruments for every dollar of assets purchased from its own capital.

An alternative measure of leverage is the *debt-to-assets* ratio. The idea behind this substitute measure is that it shows directly the proportion of assets that are funded by debt rather than equity. Since assets equal debt plus equity, this measure is essentially equivalent to the debt-to-equity ratio. IBM's debt-to-assets ratio at the end of 1985 was 0.39-to-1; 39 percent of its assets were raised by way of debt, and the remaining 61 percent by way of capital.

Regardless of which leverage measure is used, a point from the previous chapter deserves repeating here: A company's book value of equity may differ sharply from its market value of equity. Based on its 1985 year-end book value of $32 billion, IBM's debt-to-equity ratio was 0.64-to-1; based on its market value of $92 billion, its debt-to-equity ratio was only 0.22-to-1. If IBM was conservatively leveraged based on its 1985 book value, it was still more conservatively leveraged based on its market value.

COMPARED TO WHAT?

So, the business can track its performance along a broad front of financial ratio indicators. Exhibit 6-1 summarizes those indicators.

Having calculated these ratios from the income statement and balance sheet data, the manager is left with the question, "Compared to what?" The ratios have no value by themselves To be useful as a basis for effective action, they should be held up against appropriate standards: industry norms, company targets, historical ranges, or simply rules of thumb.

Industry norms provide an appropriate standard for comparison for most businesses. Inventory turnover in the restaurant business is considerably higher than in the antique furniture business, and the owner of each type of establishment interested in controlling inventory turnover would want to examine the numbers for his or her business against comparable ones from similar establishments. Several organizations (including Dun & Bradstreet, Moody's Investor Service, Robert Morris Associates, and Standard & Poor's) provide financial ratio data for a fairly wide variety of major industry groups.

Let's look at IBM's financial ratios and compare them to the computer manufacturing industry as a whole. Since IBM captures about 70 percent of the profit of the entire industry,

EXHIBIT 6-1
Financial Ratios for Assessing the Firm's Profitability and Solvency

Profitability Ratios:

1. Stockholder's Return on Investment = (Dividends + Capital Gains) as a % of Investment Outlay
2. Principal's Return on Investment = (Share of Business Profit + Salary + Extras) as a % of (Investment Outlay + Market Value of Time)
3. Earnings per Share = After-tax Profit / No. Shares of Stock Outstanding
4. Return on Stockholders' Equity = After-tax Profit / Average Stockholders' Equity
5. Gross Profit Margin = Gross Profit as a % of Sales
6. Operating Profit Margin = Operating Profit as a % of Sales
7. Net Profit Margin = Net Profit as a % of Sales

Liquidity (Short-term Solvency) Ratios:

8. Current Ratio = Current Assets / Current Liabilities
9. Quick (or "Acid Test") Ratio = (Current Assets − Inventory) / Current Liabilities
10. Average Collection Period (in days) = (Average Accounts Receivable / Annual Revenue) × 365
11. Average Payables Period (in days) = (Average Accounts Payable / Annual Cost of Sales) × 365
12. Inventory Turnover = Cost of Sales / Average Inventory

Financial Leverage (Long-term Solvency) Ratios:

13. Debt to Equity = Total Liabilities / Equity
14. Debt to Assets = Total Liabilities / Total Assets

---

we should not be too surprised to learn that the company's financial ratios stack up pretty well against the norms of the industry. Exhibit 6-2 provides such a comparison.

The most substantial differences between IBM's ratios and those for the rest of the industry are in the profitability category. In terms of both earnings per share and return on equity, IBM was significantly more profitable than the competition in 1985.

IBM was slightly more liquid than the industry as a whole in 1985, with a current ratio more than 10 percent above the com-

EXHIBIT 6-2
Selected Financial Ratios for IBM and the Competition
Fiscal Year 1985

	IBM	Other Computer Manufacturers
Profitability Ratios: *		
Earnings per Share	$10.67	$0.66
Return on Equity	22.4%	11.7%
Net Profit Margin	13.1%	3.7%
Liquidity Ratios: **		
Current Ratio	2.3 : 1	2.0 : 1
Quick Ratio	1.5 : 1	1.1 : 1
Average Collection Period (days)	70	64
Average Payables Period (days)	30	43
Inventory Turnover	2.0	3.6
Financial Leverage Ratios: **		
Debt to Equity	0.64 : 1	1.1 : 1
Debt to Assets	0.39 : 1	0.52 : 1

Source: Standard & Poor's Industry Surveys (Nov. 6, 1985).
**Source:* Robert Morris Associates' *Annual Statement Studies* (September 1986). Data from financial statements for 12 months ending between 6/30/85 and 3/31/86.

petition. Of course, with its enormously higher profitability over the years, it could afford to be more liquid.

The company was also financially more conservative than its competition, raising the vast majority of funds for its assets by way of capital (61 percent) rather than debt (39 percent). The rest of the computer industry relied less heavily on capital (48 percent) than debt (52 percent).

Do these numbers provide either IBM or the rest of the computer manufacturing industry with information that is useful for managing? You bet they do. Each company, knowing the numbers, can see more precisely where it stands in relation to the competition. Each can be more knowledgeable about its liquidity—the size of its cash and other working capital balances, bill collection and payment policies, and inventory management policies. Each can be more conscious about its financial leverage—decisions to raise funds by way of additional loans rather than additional capital. And possibly as a result of this enhanced awareness, each may streamline its operations and become more profitable.

There is no guarantee, however, that watching the ratios will lead inevitably to more profit. The ratios say nothing about changes in the underlying industry and larger economic conditions that can profoundly influence the firm's financial success. Nor do they attend specifically to the myriad individual factors that can cause the firm to either take off or fail financially: the quality of the management team, a patent to an extremely popular product, the entry of a major new competitor into the firm's market, a huge liability suit against the company, and so on.

From the individual firm's vantage point, one good reason to target ratios other than those of the industry is that the entire industry may be off base. In 1945, J. Peter Grace took over a tired shipping company founded by his grandfather and eventually converted it into a totally different, and substantially more profitable, business. He didn't accomplish that by trying to bring the financial ratios for W.R. Grace & Company closer into line with those of the shipping industry.

Even when the industry is doing well, an individual firm may not wish to aim at industry ratios. Some businesses just don't fall neatly into any of the publishers' industry groupings. Others are uniquely situated such that the industry norm is just not an appropriate standard. IBM should not aim toward industry-wide ratios, nor should any other firm that is surpassing the performance of its industry as a whole—as long as the firm is conscious about its departures from the norms and clear about how those departures contribute to the firm's higher profitability! Other businesses, because of their unique markets, locations, arrangements with suppliers, the depths of their owners' pockets, or perhaps because of their nonprofit objectives, might also have good reason to merely be aware of the industry norms, but not use them as targets.

Regardless of whether or not the firm chooses to adopt industry norms as its own set of standards of financial performance, the norms should be extremely useful to the firm as guideposts as it develops its own financial plans and its specific budgets. The alternative of ignoring industry norms, often the product of arrogance, ignorance, preoccupation with other pressing problems, and so on, can in time cause the bank to close the firm's doors. According to Sanford Jacobs, columnist and reporter for *The Wall Street Journal*,

Accountants see it all the time—management by ignorance. An owner doesn't realize his business is in trouble until it is too late. . . . Seat-of-the-pants operators fail to monitor all aspects of their businesses. They tend to think everything is fine if sales are increasing and there is money in the bank.*

Financial ratios, in short, provide a rough-and-ready set of indicators that go far beyond the monitoring of sales and the amount of money in the bank, and they are easily derived from the firm's basic financial statements. When combined with more detailed analyses of business segments, described in the two previous chapters, and with cash flow projections, described in the next chapter, these ratios can provide the business with a quick and fairly reliable basis for the diagnosis and treatment of its well-being.

*Sanford L. Jacobs, "Watch the Numbers to Learn If the Business is Doing Well," *The Wall Street Journal* (August 26, 1985), p. 19.

7

MANAGING CASH FLOW

The only irreparable mistake in business is to run out of cash. Almost any other mistake in business can be remedied in one way or another. But when you run out of cash, they take you out of the game.

—HAROLD GENEEN

Profits are the bottom line of the income statement and the best single measure of the firm's performance, but many an owner of a profitable, growing business has lost his company for lack of cash. The juggling act of management consists of keeping aloft not only the bowling pins of the business that determine its profit and the twirling torches that determine its growth, but also the spinning knives that determine its cash balances. Successful managers of growing businesses learn to keep track of the whole act. If they drop the knives, the rest will come tumbling down, too.

THE BASICS: CASH, CASH FLOW, AND WORKING CAPITAL

Managing the flow of cash begins with knowing what it is. *Cash* is the medium of exchange that allows the firm to do business

83

—it is the life blood of the firm's operations. As an item on the balance sheet, cash consists of the firm's checking and savings account balances, currency on hand (petty cash), and a few other holdings that vendors readily accept in exchange for goods and services, such as money market accounts with check drafting privileges.

Cash flow refers to the dynamics of the firm's cash balances— the amount of cash that it generates and uses. The difference between cash and cash flow is essentially like the difference between the balance sheet and the income statement; the former has to do with dollar amounts or balances at a *point* in time, and the latter has to do with changes in dollar amounts *over* time.

Since cash flow management is really about managing the firm's short-term solvency, it is important to look not just at changes in cash balances, but at changes in other liquid assets as well, especially *working capital*—the value of resources that are quickly converted into cash (current assets) less short-term obligations that draw against cash (current liabilities). Managing short-term solvency is about managing both the firm's cash and its other liquid assets as well.

HOW THE FIRM CREATES AND USES CASH

Two of the basics of cash flow are obvious to most managers: (1) the firm's cash balance declines when the firm uses more cash than it generates, and it grows when the opposite is true; and (2) sales generate cash, and cash gets used up in the purchase of goods for sale, payroll, rent, utilities, and other expenses. Those basics are useful, but hopelessly inadequate. There's a whole lot more to cash flow than sales and expenses.

To really understand all of the ways that cash can be created or expended, it helps to recall the basic balance sheet equation:

$$\text{Assets} = \text{Liabilities} + \text{Equity.} \qquad (1)$$

Now, assets can be divided into two parts—cash and all other assets—so we can restate equation (1) as:

$$\text{Cash} + \text{Noncash Assets} = \text{Liabilities} + \text{Equity.} \qquad (2)$$

Next, to see what determines the firm's cash balance, we subtract noncash assets from both sides of equation (2):

$$\text{Cash} = \text{Liabilities} + \text{Equity} - \text{Noncash Assets.} \qquad (3)$$

This equation indicates that the company's cash balance can be expanded by increasing liabilities (i.e., by taking out or extending a loan), increasing equity (increasing retained earnings or issuing stock), or by selling assets.

The least harmful of these options to the business is usually that of increasing equity through retained earnings—making a profit. The alternatives can be costly: Expanding liabilities means incurring added interest expense and increasing the risk of bankruptcy; expanding equity other than retained earnings usually means giving up either control of the business or one's own personal resources for the sake of the business; and selling assets usually means reducing the firm's potential for making future profits.

Since cash is best increased through profit, and since profit is hidden within the equity component of equation (3), it is easier to see how cash balances are fully determined by replacing the equity item with its components—retained earnings and stocks:

$$\text{Cash} = \text{Liabilities} + \text{Retained Earnings} \\ + \text{Stocks} - \text{Noncash Assets.} \qquad (4)$$

Finally, since the retained earnings item consists of accumulated revenues minus accumulated expenses, we can restate equation (4) by replacing retained earnings by those components:

$$\text{Cash} = \text{Liabilities} + \text{Stocks} + \text{Revenues}$$
$$- \text{Expenses} - \text{Noncash Assets}. \qquad (5)$$

This last equation summarizes all the ways—the *only* ways—that cash can be increased:

By increasing debt

By issuing stock

By generating sales and collecting nonoperating income (interest)

By reducing costs

By converting accounts receivable and other noncash assets into cash.

Later in this chapter we will see that these sources and uses of cash serve as the basis for reports that are indispensable to managers who want to anticipate cash needs and control cash flow. Before we do that, we can look at some common manifestations of cash flow problems in the real world, problems that those reports are designed to avert.

THE ANATOMY OF A CASH CRISIS

All businesses face crises, sometimes on a daily basis. Real crisis exists when the firm runs out of cash. When the company doesn't have enough cash to pay vendors of needed goods or services, the vendors may be tolerant for a while, but eventually they'll stop supplying the company and, in time, may sue for payment, forcing the company into bankruptcy. Or the firm may be able to hold off the vendors, but miss a payroll, in which case the employees usually quit and the firm is no longer regarded as a going concern by either the vendors or the clients—another route to the bankruptcy court.

This happens eventually to most chronically unprofitable companies, along lines such as these: (1) successive losses cause the erosion of the firm's equity cushion; (2) management seeks various sources of investment capital or bank financing, but is unwilling to give up control of the company for the capital and is turned down by the banks because of the firm's poor performance record; (3) the firm is then forced to draw down its cash accounts to perilous levels while management attempts desperately to generate more revenues and hold off the creditors (typically claiming a temporary cash flow ailment rather than a more fundamental disease); and (4) eventually, the firm fails to meet a payroll, or the bank demands payment on a delinquent note, or a creditor sues the firm for nonpayment.

The cash crisis can happen also to the firm with a voracious appetite for growth. The Osborne Computer Corporation skyrocketed to success in 1982 on the strength of its then technically innovative and low-priced Osborne 1 portable computer. The company's founder and chief executive officer, Adam Osborne, brimming with the hubris of extraordinary growth of his firm's revenues and profits—which appeared at the time to pose a legitimate threat to IBM, Apple Computer, and the rest of the microcomputer market—built up his company's production capacity sharply on the expectation that the steep growth in revenues and profits of 1982 would continue for some time.

Then, in March 1983, Osborne announced that the successor to the Osborne 1 computer, the Osborne Executive, would be available in June. The announcement caused prospective buyers of Osborne computers to put off their purchases until the new model was available, but the company failed to meet its planned June availability date by several months. In the meantime, production costs continued to surge, quickly eroding the company's modest equity and cash cushions. In September 1983 the firm filed for protection from creditors under Chapter 11 bankruptcy, and its assets were eventually liquidated.

Osborne's fatal error was his March announcement; the firm's cash position became hopeless not long afterward. Growth is wonderful when all goes as planned, but in this case the plans, and the firm's reserves, were simply inadequate. Osborne's primary claim to distinction in the annals of computerdom turned out not to be the emergence of his company into the Fortune 500. Adam Osborne has come to be remembered largely for his horrendous miscalculation, the inability of his company to sustain even a short-term setback in its ambitious growth plan due to insufficient equity and cash reserves, and the rapid downfall of the Osborne Computer Corporation that resulted.

KEY TO CASH MANAGEMENT: UNDERSTANDING THE FIRM'S PRIOR CASH FLOW

Avoiding a cash crisis starts with knowing how the firm obtains and uses cash. Historical cash flows, while frequently unlike future cash flows, nonetheless provide a useful point of departure for anticipating the firm's cash needs and controlling its cash flow, and thus keeping the company solvent.

The accounting profession provides a report, the *statement of changes in financial position*, that gives management such information. The statement shows the firm's sources and uses of liquidity during an accounting period, generally on a cash, funds, or working capital basis. Exhibit 7-1 shows this information for IBM on a funds basis, where IBM's accountants define funds as cash plus marketable securities. IBM calls the report its "consolidated statement of funds flow." (The term *funds* has created some confusion among accountants and nonaccountants alike. Generally, it means liquid assets; in actual practice, the term is arbitrarily defined to include various combinations of liquid resources ranging from cash alone to working capital.)

Note first that Exhibit 7-1 reveals that during 1985 IBM's cash and marketable securities balances grew by 29 percent, a total of $1.26 billion. You can look at IBM's balance sheets for year-ends 1984 and 1985 and see, indeed, that cash grew by $296 million and marketable securities grew by $964 million during 1985, which provides comforting agreement with Exhibit 7-1. Comforting agreement, however, is not the same as useful information. Those responsible for managing IBM's liquidity need much more than successive balance sheets can offer.

The statement of changes in financial position is designed to provide more. It shows that IBM's liquidity position grew by nearly 30 percent primarily on the strength of the company's $6.6 billion of net profit after taxes. Depreciation was the second largest contributor to IBM's liquidity, at more than $3 billion. (Why does depreciation contribute to cash? Because, as an expense, it reduces the profit figure on the line above, but does so without drawing down cash, so it must get added back in; if the line above were based only on expenses that used cash, we wouldn't have to show depreciation and amortization as contributors to cash.) The largest draw against IBM's liquidity in 1985 was investment in plant and other property, followed by the company's purchase of inventory and its payment of dividends to the corporate stockholders.

IBM's "funds flow" statement also shows the mix of added liquidity that came from operations (68 percent), from debt financing (29 percent), and from the issue of new stocks (3 percent).

In short, the statement of changes in financial position provides an accurate picture of how the company's liquidity has changed. It gives the historical facts that set the foundation for accurate projections of the firm's future cash flows.

EXHIBIT 7-1
Statement of Changes in Financial Position
International Business Machines Corporation
For the year ending December 31, 1985
($ Millions)

Funds (Cash & Marketable Securities) on January 1		$4,362
Funds from (used for) Operations:		
SOURCES:		
Net Profit After Taxes	$ 6,555	
Depreciation of Plant	157	
Other Depreciation Expenses	2,894	
Property Retired or Sold	867	
Amortization of Software	425	
Deferred Income Taxes & Other	1,880	
	$12,778	
USES:		
Investment in Rental Machines	$ 313	
Investment in Program Products	785	
Investment in Other Property	6,117	
Realized Appreciation of Assets	454	
Net Increase in Working Capital Other than Cash, Marketable Securities, & Loans Payable	3,101	
Translation Effects	(677)	
	$10,093	
Net Funds From Operations		$2,685
Funds from External Financing:		
Net Increase in Long-term Debt	$ 686	
Net Increase in Loans Payable	459	
Net Funds from External Financing		$1,145
Funds from Employee & Stockholder Plan		133
Less Cash Dividends Paid		2,703
Funds (Cash & Marketable Securities) on December 31		$5,622

PROJECTING CASH BALANCES

Having built such an historical base, how does the manager protect the firm's short-term solvency? By planning and controlling the firm's sources and uses of cash. At the heart of the planning aspect of cash flow management are accurate cash forecasts.

Before seeing how the cash flow projection process actually works, it's worth looking at the importance of accurate projections of cash flow in more tangible terms. Accurate projections serve the cause of cash flow planning, but planning is no end in itself. There are three solid reasons for accurate projections of cash flow:

1. they allow the firm's managers to anticipate and satisfy cash needs in advance and thereby avoid cash flow crises;

2. when given to banks or other financial institutions, accurate projections of cash flow induce those institutions to give better terms than the terms that prevail when companies attempt to negotiate short-term loans either with poorly conceived plans or at the moment of crisis; and

3. they enable the firm to anticipate periods of excess cash reserves so that investment opportunities can be more systematically exploited.

Suppose your company has set up a structure of general ledger accounts that clearly identifies all the firm's major operational segments, and suppose that it has produced accurate and informative balance sheets, income statements, and statements of changes in financial position. Now you want to manage cash flow. How do you forecast sources and uses of cash, say, for each of the next three months?

The best place to begin is where you are: your firm's current cash balance, its current receivables and payables and the aging distribution of each, business currently in the pipeline (any commitments that do not show up as receivables or payables), and operating expenses. On this base of certainties and near certainties you build your best estimates of the additional revenues that your company expects over each of the next three months, and the costs associated with those revenues.

The accuracy of your cash flow projections will depend substantially on the accuracy of these estimates of revenues and costs of goods sold, and detailed estimates tend to be more accurate, so the estimates should be detailed. More important, the solvency and survival of your company may be in jeopardy if the revenue projections are too generous or the cost projections shortsighted, so the estimates should also be conservative. Such estimates should come out of the firm's operating budget for the coming quarter, which will be discussed in some detail in the next chapter.

The resulting cash flow projection, if it is to be an effective management tool, should be more detailed than the firm's statement of changes in financial position, an historical record, primarily in the following ways:

1. rather than simply showing profit as the first source of cash, the projection should itemize revenue expected by business segment as sources of cash and costs of goods sold expected by segment and expected operating expenses by account (salaries, rent, utilities, etc.) as uses of cash; and

2. cash from receivables (and for payables) for each month or week should be itemized in terms of collections (payments) expected from receivables (for debts) that will be up to 30 days old, those that will be from 31 to 60 days old, 61 to 90 days old, and more than 90 days old.

The cost projections usually begin with an estimate of the cost of goods sold, the largest component of total costs for most companies. Cost of goods sold are typically estimated as a percentage of revenues, adjusted for any anticipated extraordinary circumstances, such as a large-volume purchase of raw material to exploit a one-time discount opportunity. In projecting other costs, it's best to rely on those in the company who make or influence the spending decisions, especially in such areas as expenditures on plant and equipment, either for growth or replacement, and marketing costs for major advertising campaigns.

The basic format for the cash flow projection is shown in Exhibit 7-2. A good projection will be much more detailed about revenues and costs than the one shown. Since the point of this projection is to establish whether there will be enough (or too much) cash in the company over the near term, the bottom line of this report, literally and figuratively, is the firm's cash balance at the end of the period.

It's not a bad idea to check the initial cash flow projection against the firm's statement of changes in financial position for the same month or quarter last year to ensure that nothing important has been overlooked. If there's very little seasonal fluctuation in the firm's financial numbers, you can check your projections against the statement of changes in financial position for the most recent month or quarter instead.

If reliable cash flow projections show a negative balance, or even a small positive one, that's generally a signal for immediate action. What kind of action? These are the basic options: (1) expanding external financing, either debt or equity; (2) increasing payables by paying later; (3) generating more sales than predicted; (4) reducing costs below the level predicted; and (5) converting assets to cash—especially collecting receivables faster.

The option or combination of options for increasing cash balances that is best for a particular firm will depend on a variety of factors. One is the extent to which the firm has already used each option—at some point, banks will no longer extend credit to a highly leveraged firm, creditors won't be put off any

EXHIBIT 7-2
Quarterly Cash Flow Projection

	Month 1	Month 2	Month 3
Cash at start of month	$50,000	$ 60,000	$ 12,000
Cash from (used for) operations:			
SOURCES:			
Cash revenues—goods	$10,000	$ 15,000	$ 15,000
Cash revenues—services	5,000	10,000	10,000
30-day receivables collected	20,000	25,000	25,000
31- to 60-day receivables	10,000	10,000	15,000
61- to 90-day receivables	5,000	5,000	5,000
>90-day receivables	5,000	5,000	5,000
Depreciation & amortization	1,000	1,000	2,000
Property sold	0	0	10,000
	$56,000	$ 71,000	$ 87,000
USES:			
Cost of goods sold	$30,000	$ 35,000	$ 35,000
Cost of services	3,000	6,000	6,000
Operating expenses	10,000	12,000	12,000
Taxes	1,000	0	0
Investment in assets	5,000	65,000	65,000
Realized appreciation	0	0	5,000
	$49,000	$118,000	$123,000
Net cash from operations	$ 7,000	$ (47,000)	$ (36,000)
Less cash dividends paid	3,000	$ 0	$ 0
Cash from external financing:			
Net increase in current debt	$ 1,000	$ (1,000)	$ 5,000
Net increase in long-term debt	5,000	0	25,000
Net increase in equity	0	0	25,000
Cash from external sources	$ 6,000	$ (1,000)	$ 55,000
Cash at end of month	$60,000	$ 12,000	$ 31,000

longer, debtors can't be pressured any more intensely to pay up, costs can't be reduced further, and so on. The option chosen will depend also on how quickly the firm needs the cash and how long it will take to carry out each option; getting cash from external sources, for example, usually takes longer than the other options. How the firm should increase cash will depend also on the effect of each option on the firm's profitability; the option of raising cash by selling assets, for example, usually hurts profits to a greater extent than does the option of acquiring fresh capital. Fresh capital, however, can come at the expense of yet another factor that will be more critical to some firms than others: the risk that that option will cause loss of control of the company.

The firm shown in Exhibit 7-2 is a growing engineering firm, in need of additional workstations for its engineers in order to maintain its profitability and continue its growth. It appears to have enough cash to purchase a $65,000 workstation for Month 2, but must obtain $50,000 of additional financing before it can purchase another workstation in Month 3. As a rule, the firm's managers can obtain that sort of information only by projecting cash flow in the general manner shown in the exhibit.

The numbers of this example, in fact, suggest the need for a more in-depth, weekly forecast of cash flow, at least for Month 2. Even if the numbers shown are completely accurate, the $12,000 cash balance at the end of the month may hide the fact that the expenses may concentrate in the first two weeks of the month, while the revenues are likely to show up toward the end of the month. If so, the workstation should be purchased toward the end of the month rather than early in the month.

Once the cash flow projection is agreed upon as complete and sound by the firm's managers, it can become the plan that guides the firm's operations over the short term. As emergencies and unforeseeable opportunities emerge, of course, it may become necessary to change the plan.

HOW MUCH CASH IS ENOUGH?

An obvious solution to the problem of tight cash flow is simply to maintain a permanently large cash balance. After all, why should the company have to either risk a cash crisis or go to the trouble of developing detailed financial projections? A large cash balance can eliminate both the risk of insolvency and the need for such careful planning. Many managers do not have the temperament either for bearing such risks or for engaging in detailed planning.

The executives of many firms, in fact, choose to have large cash balances precisely to avoid such risks and needs. In so choosing, however, they deprive the firm of profitable uses of cash. Even when the firm cannot expect a profitable return on investments in additional assets that it might purchase and place in operation, the firm can usually do better than to keep large amounts of cash in an interest-bearing checking account or money fund. Government securities, certificates of deposits, and commercial paper all yield higher returns and are essentially riskless. Shifting relatively unproductive cash to such instruments, however, means that the cash is no longer available to the company as needed without a substantial penalty. Investing cash in such a way effectively requires that the firm manage its cash flow, whether it likes to or not.

Publicly traded firms that choose to maintain large cash balances bring upon themselves a potentially graver problem than reduced profitability: They risk being taken over by larger, cash-hungry institutions. Corporations with lots of cash tend to become targets of hostile takeovers by organizations in need of cash. While such takeovers often bring about hefty increases in the price of the stock, the former executives of the company taken over are usually let go. It's not called hostile for nothing.

Precisely how much cash the company should keep in reserve depends on several factors. The firm should maintain smaller cash reserve balances if its managers can project cash flow fairly accurately, if it can put cash to more profitable uses, if it has assets that can be quickly converted to cash without great expense, and if its managers can tolerate some risk of a cash crisis.

Whatever level of cash reserves the managers choose, it's

generally best to express that choice as an acceptable range rather than a precise single amount. Projections of cash balances usually diverge from actual cash balances unevenly from one period to the next, so it's normal for the cash reserves to fluctuate over time.

Ultimately, the right amount of cash is a matter of experience and taste. The job of the firm's financial managers is simply to remain conscious of the firm's cash, so that they can know when to create cash and how much to create, and when to engage cash in profitable uses and how much to engage.

8

BUDGETING FOR PROFIT: PLANNING AND CONTROL OF FINANCIAL SUCCESS

Budgets are not merely affairs of arithmetic, but in a thousand ways go to the root of prosperity of individuals, the relation of classes and the strength of kingdoms.

—WILLIAM E. GLADSTONE

Firms that are consistently profitable generally have more than good luck on their side. They usually have someone at the top who knows how to anticipate events and control the destiny of the organization. The chairman of the board of one major corporation put it this way: "There is nothing that a chief executive likes less than to be surprised."* Most chief executives avoid surprises through thoughtful planning and conscientious execution and control.

*Thomas H. Wyman, Chairman of CBS, speech at Dickinson College, quoted in *The Wall Street Journal* (April 30, 1986), p. 32. Louis Pasteur made a similar observation about a century earlier: "Chance favors only the prepared mind."

Wyman was less than successful at anticipating events and controlling the destiny of his own organization; the CBS board of directors, unhappy with his performance after months of internal turmoil, accepted his resignation on September 10, 1986.

Surprise avoidance is not the only good reason to engage seriously in the planning and control process. An equally important reason is to improve communication and induce alignment among the firm's managers and employees. Effective planning and control requires that the people at the top: (1) tell others in the organization their vision of the company, and (2) ask others for specifics as to how that vision can become reality. It then requires that those specifics be developed. All of which is precisely the kind of communication that should occur in a company, if it is to be profitable. It might occur anyway, but the process of planning and control can make it happen in settings where it would not otherwise.

The most important reason of all for planning and control, however, is neither avoiding surprise nor improving communication. The primary purpose of planning and control is to clarify the goals of the organization and to enhance the prospect of achieving them. Profitable firms generally plan for their profits.

How do they do it? Successful business planning generally proceeds along a path that includes the steps shown in Exhibit 8-1. Let's look at each of those steps in detail.

THE BASICS: DEFINING THE BUSINESS, STATING GOALS AND ASSUMPTIONS

Defining the Business. Planning begins with primitive inquiry: What is our firm about—what business are we in? What are our firm's primary products and services? Whom does it serve?

IBM defines its business right at the beginning of its annual report:

IBM's operations are primarily in the field of information-handling systems, equipment and services to solve the increasingly complex problems of business, government, science, space ex-

EXHIBIT 8-1
Elements of Planning and Control

1. Define the business, state goals and assumptions
2. Develop a strategic plan
3. Develop a baseline forecast
4. Identify alternative business strategies
5. Analyze alternatives and select one
6. Develop a plan and a corresponding operating budget
7. Develop control and adjustment procedures
8. Obtain commitments
9. Execute

ploration, defense, education, medicine and many other areas of human activity. IBM's products include information processing products and systems, program products, telecommunications systems, office systems, typewriters, copiers, educational and testing materials, and related supplies and services. Most products are both leased and sold through IBM's worldwide marketing organizations. Selected products are marketed and distributed through authorized dealers and remarketers.*

IBM, in short, is in the business of solving complex problems, especially those that lend themselves to information technology solutions; it produces information processing products and services; and its market includes virtually every type of organization, public and private, as well as a broad cross section of individuals.

Stating Goals and Assumptions

Given the answers to such fundamental questions about the business and its primary markets, the next basic question can be asked: What are the goals of the business? A primary goal of

*International Business Machines Corporation, *Annual Report* (1985).

virtually all profit-making organizations is to make a profit
—the more, the better. Other goals, often equally important to
the principals of the firm, include: business growth, creation of
goodwill, and eventual capital gain; market dominance; contribution to the firm's clients, to its employees, and to the community. (See Exhibit 8–2.)

It's best to express those goals in specific terms: increase
profit this year by 25 percent over last year; increase assets by
20 percent; increase market share of the firm's primary product
from 5 to 15 percent this year and to 50 percent in five years;
bring an important new product to the market by June 1; build
return on investment steadily to 20 percent in five years and 25
percent in 10; and so on.

Notice that the goals are expressed in terms of *tangible* results
to be attained within *specific* time periods. Discipline is the essential characteristic of the consistently profitable firm; stating
goals in such explicit terms generally helps to impose such discipline and make success more likely.

Notice also that some goals are for the coming year and others are for the long term. What is meant by long term? That de-

EXHIBIT 8-2
Common Business Goals

1. Profitability
2. Growth
3. Market share
4. Survival
5. Image
6. Social, political influence
7. Minimize risk, disruption
8. Contribution to the firm's clients
9. Contribution to the firm's staff
10. Contribution to the community

pends on the industry. A 10-year planning horizon is too long for most firms in the computer software and high fashion design businesses, and too short for most firms in the forestry business. Whether its long-term horizon is two years or 50, the firm should also create short- and intermediate-term benchmark goals to bring some immediacy to the planning and control process.

Within the firm, top management generally assumes primary responsibility for setting and achieving the long-term goals. While top management is fully responsible for the firm's short-term goals as well, lower-level managers usually play the primary role in creating the more detailed short-term goals and plans, just as they play the primary role in executing and controlling operations within their various spheres of authority. Any discrepancies among the goals of various units within the organization should be resolved by the responsible managers.

Regardless of the firm's specific goals and planning horizon, achieving the goals will be predicated on a set of assumptions about what is likely. For example: General business conditions and trends will proceed as last year; interest rates will stay essentially flat this year, but will double within five years; the competition will continue to expand as it did last year; there will be no major changes in our suppliers; staff turnover will be about like last year; government policy that affects the business will not change fundamentally over the next five years; and so on.

Some of those assumptions may, in hindsight, turn out to be way off the mark. The economy might, for example, actually turn down sharply next year, stiff competition could emerge within two months, and the firm's primary supplier might go bankrupt. To avoid building a plan on a foundation of faulty assumptions, many companies construct three sets of assumptions: pessimistic, most likely, and optimistic. While the firm's basic plan should generally be based on the most likely set of assumptions, developing alternative sets of assumptions will inject some awareness of contingencies and, as a result, some flexibility into the planning and control process.

DEVELOPING A STRATEGIC PLAN

Having established the most elementary features of the firm —the business it's in, its goals, and basic assumptions about its future—it's time to sharpen some central aspects of its long-term plan: What are the firm's primary strengths and weaknesses? What are the key factors necessary for the firm to meet its goals? How will it adapt to changes in its external environment—changes in consumer demographics and tastes, the competition, economic conditions, and so on? Addressing such issues and developing a basic business strategy in light of the answers to those questions is what *strategic planning* is all about. The basic idea, as noted in Chapter 5, is to demystify the future of the business so that the managers can take control of events that would otherwise seem uncontrollable.

Whether the firm is primarily in the business of delivering goods or services, this inquiry can begin by comparing its current clientele with the market it has been targeting. Such a comparison might reveal that the firm's marketing efforts have cast a much broader net than is reflected by its actual clientele, suggesting that the firm might be more successful if it targeted more intensively on the specific niche in which it has already proven to be successful. Or it might reveal the opposite; if the firm has attracted customers on which it has not previously targeted its marketing efforts, it might consider widening its marketing focus to serve more of such firms in the future.

Knowing the characteristics of the firm's customer base and how they are changing is a crucial aspect of niche marketing. If the firm's products or services are used primarily by small businesses and the conditions that support small businesses are declining, the firm would do well to explore new markets. If the products or services are used primarily by middle-class young people, the firm would do well to examine whether this clientele will grow over the next few years. If the firm's primary client is a large corporation, it should carefully examine the financial health of that client and the likelihood of the client's shifting to another supplier.

It's impossible, of course, to identify each and every issue that should be addressed in the strategic planning process. Strategic planning differs from firm to firm, depending on the firm's business, size, geographic location, employee base, the competition, and countless other factors. The purpose here is to give a sense of the importance of developing a strategic plan and the basic elements of strategic planning.

DEVELOPING A BASELINE FORECAST

Having established or reestablished the firm's basic purpose and the assumptions shaping its future, it's good to project business performance for at least the coming year under those basic premises. The simplest first-cut forecast of the firm's financial performance and condition will consist of a straight-line projection of its recent income statements and balance sheets. This forecast can be done manually, but it can be done more efficiently on a personal computer with the help of an electronic spreadsheet program, preferably one with regression and graphing capabilities. (See Exhibits 8-3 and 8-4.)

The assumption of such projections is this: The recent trend of the business will continue for the coming year. This assumption is often realistic. Even when it's unrealistic, a more realistic estimate of the firm's *pro forma* (forecasted) straight-line projection is still a useful point of departure for income statements and balance sheets. The second-cut projection can adjust the

EXHIBIT 8-3
Baseline Projection of Income Statement
For Fiscal Year 19x9

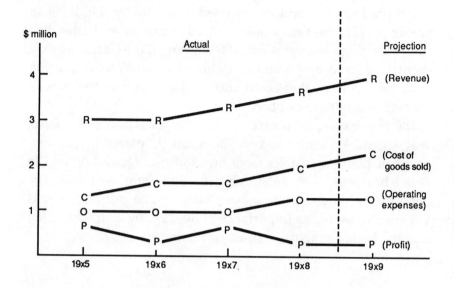

EXHIBIT 8-4
Baseline Projection of Balance Sheet
For end of Fiscal Year 19x9

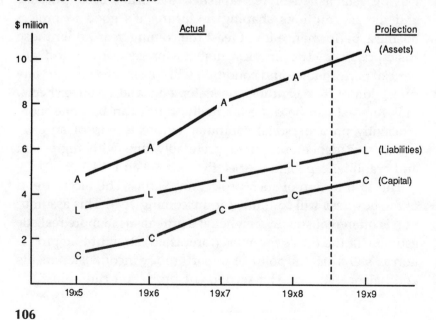

straight-line projection to reflect assumptions about recent or anticipated changes in consumer demographics and behavior, the competition, supply prices, labor market conditions, and so on. The resulting forecast of the firm's performance and condition will serve as the baseline against which alternative business strategies can be evaluated.

IDENTIFYING ALTERNATIVE BUSINESS STRATEGIES

Given this baseline projection of the company's likely future, the firm's managers must next explore alternative strategies for achieving its goals—statements of what may be possible. This phase of the planning cycle is often referred to as the what-if phase. The what-if strategies under consideration may include orthodox approaches used elsewhere in the firm or industry, approaches borrowed from other industries or settings, or approaches that are altogether different from anything conventional. While unconventional approaches tend to be more risky, they are also more often associated with major breakthroughs.

Balancing the security and limitations of the familiar with the possibilities and risks of something new is, for sure, a central problem of this phase of the planning process; it is perhaps the central problem of entrepreneurship. Successful plans are generally rooted in management's experience of what is achievable, but really successful plans extend well beyond what has been achieved. In short, this phase of the planning process calls for creativity, and that usually means letting go of conventional thought and practice. This can be extremely uncomfortable, but letting go is generally a requirement for extraordinary success. Remember, we've not yet committed the business to anything at this stage.

The process of creating more profitable alternative strategies should take on both the revenues and the costs sides of the income statement. On the revenues side, the most successful marketing strategies generally grow out of a keen sensitivity to the customer's needs. This can begin with a focused line of inquiry: What do we do best? How does that product or service satisfy the needs of the customer? What else do we do well? How does that satisfy needs? How might we satisfy those needs better—what's missing? In what ways do our current operations place our needs ahead of the clients' needs?

A particularly effective strategy for identifying profitable modifications of existing products and services, or the development or acquisition of new ones, is simply to inquire about common customer or distributor complaints. Anyone who ever complained of getting stuck by safety pins while changing the baby's diapers can appreciate the pinless disposable diapers that captured the diaper market in the 1970s. Anyone who ever complained about cans of motor oil that invariably dripped oil on the engine and garage floor can appreciate the dripless plastic oil containers that were produced in the 1980s.

The firm can elicit customer complaints in a variety of ways. Complaints should be documented as they are initiated by customers, often by way of distributors. The firm can also ask customers directly whether they have any complaints about any of the firm's products or services, either casually or systematically in the natural course of business, or by way of a special survey. Some firms offer special opportunities for customers to complain or offer suggestions by publicizing a tollfree telephone number for those purposes.

Good ideas can begin with the customer, but others usually generate good ideas, too: employees, managers, consultants, and, of course, competitors. The 3M Corporation's Post-It™ note pad was an employee's idea, one that has become the quintessential example of the concept of corporate *intra*preneurship. VisiCorp's software product, VisiCalc, was the first electronic spreadsheet, and a pretty financially successful product; but its primary claim to fame is that it was the good idea that paved the way for a vastly more successful product —Lotus Development Corporation's 1-2-3. No single participant in the process of developing profitable strategies has a monopoly on creativity.

Regardless of *who* creates the alternative strategies, certain principles apply to *how* successful strategies are created. One customer-oriented approach to generating creative product and service alternatives is to think less about how existing products and services can be modified and more about specific customer needs. Velcro®, widely used to quickly secure flaps on clothing, luggage, handbags and wallets, harnesses, sporting and camping gear, and an infinite variety of industrial items is obviously not the result of an inquiry about how the zipper could be modified; it operates in a way that bears no resemblance to the zipper's operation. Nor did videotapes and VCRs for widespread home use result from thinking about how the movie camera and projector could be improved.

A conventional and often effective way of unearthing product and service modifications that are potentially profitable is through the use of market research. Even the most carefully done market surveys can, however, yield strategies that are extremely unprofitable. The Ford Motor Company's notorious Edsel line of the late 1950s and early 1960s resulted from a survey that unambiguously identified a strong market for such a car. The survey, unfortunately, did not anticipate that consumers would not be attracted to the name of the car or to a quirk of its grille design, which once induced Bob Hope to refer to the Edsel on prime-time network television as "an Oldsmobile sucking a lemon."

Strategies for increasing profits come as often on the side of cost control as on the side of revenue generation. Here, too, major breakthroughs result more often from thinking radically and creatively ("Suppose we eliminate our computing center") than from thinking incrementally ("Suppose we reduce operat-

CREATING NEW IDEAS AT THE WALT DISNEY COMPANY

Walt Disney was surely one of mankind's more creative thinkers. Unfortunately, his death in 1966 left Walt Disney Productions in a crisis of creativity. While revenues from the theme parks that Disney had created grew steadily for 20 years after he died, other important segments of Disney's company became stagnant and unprofitable.

The Walt Disney Studios in particular, once a pioneer in filmmaking fantasy for children and the family, was generating over $30 million in losses by 1983—ironically, while other studios were making fortunes off of *ET, Star Wars, Raiders of the Lost Ark*, and other movies that had clearly benefited from Disney's rich legacy of make-believe, idealism, and special effects. Long since written off by Hollywood, Walt Disney Productions was falling into some disfavor on Wall Street as well.

In 1984, Walt Disney's nephew, Roy, engineered the recruitment of Michael Eisner from Paramount Pictures to the Disney company as chairman of the board, and Frank Wells, formerly with Warner Brothers, as president. Eisner and Wells quickly brought in motion picture and television talent; entered the television syndication business; and created a variety of TV programs for each of the three major networks. In short order, the company was once again producing hit movies (e.g., *Down and Out in Beverly Hills, The Color of Money*, and *Ruthless People*) and TV series (e.g., *The Golden Girls*).

The company was also producing much more profit. Net income grew from $93 million in 1983 ($98 million in 1984) to $173 million in 1985, and $247 million in 1986. Earnings per share nearly tripled during the same period: from $0.68 in 1983 and 1984 to $1.29 in 1985, and $1.82 in 1986.

Eisner and Wells, of course, might have been lucky; they undoubtedly benefited in part from actions taken by their predecessors, actions that included the continued expansion of Epcot Center and the creation of a Disney cable TV channel.

Others attribute their success to creative thinking. For example, Mark Potts and Peter Behr, in their book, *The Leading Edge*, report that within days after his appointment as chairman,

Eisner gathered six of the company's most creative talents for a Sunday morning meeting at his house that within a few hours produced three ideas for Saturday morning cartoon series—a potentially lucrative field in which the company, for all its reputation as a cartoon maker, had never participated. "You've got to gather the people and then you've got to get them all excited and come up with the ideas," Eisner says.

Potts and Behr report that Wells took similar action to create new marketing ideas. At an otherwise uneventful meeting with the company's marketing staff, Wells recalls saying, "This is not a satisfactory meeting. We're going to come back tomorrow, you 15 people, and I want each of you to have at least one idea." The next day, they presented him with more than 40 ideas on how to sell the theme parks to the public, each idea "new and fresh and different" (e.g., road shows featuring Disney characters to promote the theme parks and publicity about a new 800 telephone number for park information).

Eisner and Wells were creative in other ways, too. They cut questionable projects that had been draining significant corporate resources; made Disney classics like *Pinocchio* and *Sleeping Beauty* available in videocassette format; hired Michael Jackson, George Lucas, Bette Midler, and other bankable talents for Disney projects; entered into an agreement with French officials to build a "Euro Disneyland" at a site near Paris; and supported a new generation of highly adaptable sets in Disney's theme parks designed around flexible facades and easily changed software, rather than the conventional fixed sets. They've been creative financially, too, raising hundreds of millions of dollars to finance movies through limited partnerships, and adding an estimated $150 million or so annually to the bottom line by increasing admission prices to its theme parks by 45 percent in their first two years at the helm.

It remains to be seen whether the spurt in Disney's profits in the mid-1980s will continue. Corporations are frequently accused of sacrificing long-term profitability for profits in the near-term; under Eisner and Wells, the corporation reduced capital spending from $291 million in 1983 to $179 million in 1985 at a time when dollars didn't go nearly so far—Disneyland cost only $17 million to open in 1955, while the Epcot Center cost $1.2 bil-

> lion to open in 1982. Such a reduction clearly involves a healthy degree of fat-trimming; it may also involve a degree of reduced future profits.
>
> In the meantime, however, Eisner and Wells have certainly eliminated the monotony that dwelled in the house of Disney during the 20 years since the ending of the reign of the master. Their actions have revived significant aspects of the creative Disney spirit that made the company great in the first place.

ing expenses across the board by five percent and change suppliers"). Creative cost control strategies may consist of radical reductions in both operating expenses ("Suppose we replace our 20-year-old in-house accounting bureaucracy with a minimal staff and greater reliance on an outside service that specializes in businesses like ours"), and the cost of goods sold ("Suppose we purchase our primary components from abroad rather than build them ourselves").

Among the most creative cost control strategies are those that kill the company's sacred cows. The typical example is the termination of a product or service line that has been long regarded as the firm's hope for the future, but that has yet to show the profits that were predicted at some earlier time. To identify creative cost control alternatives, try focusing on the costs of producing the unprofitable good or service and ask the following questions: What have we assumed about the consumer, the distributor, and the competition that has been incorrect? Can the product or service be inexpensively modified in a fundamental way so that the erroneous assumption gets handled? What return on investment can be expected from an alternative allocation of the resources that we use up to produce the good or provide the service?

The Apple Computer Corporation's Lisa computer, a 32-bit microcomputer with powerful graphical capabilities, was introduced in 1983 as a blockbuster technological breakthrough that would destroy the existing 16-bit microcomputer competition

—including the IBM PC. Steven Jobs, then Apple's chief executive officer and widely regarded as Silicon Valley's leading guru, assumed that the customer would be willing to pay $10,000 for such a machine. He was wrong. It became clear that the 16-bit IBM computer technology was not a passing fancy, and the Lisa turned out to be much more a cost center for Apple than a profit center. Before long, Apple acknowledged its miscalculation and created a scaled-down version of the Lisa, which it called the MacIntosh. Priced at about a third of the original price of the Lisa, the MacIntosh turned out to become one of Job's stunning successes. The road to profits is not always as straight as we map it out. Profit centers that turn out primarily to be cost centers provide the occasion to rethink the basic assumptions of the company's plan so that truly profitable alternatives can be created.

Perhaps the most effective approach to cost control is to subject the firm's operations to detailed analysis. For most businesses, labor is the most substantial cost, and opportunities to reduce those costs—and often to increase productivity—can be discovered by having each person keep a log, for at least a typical week or so, of how much time he or she spends on each task performed. Analysis of these logs can turn up areas of the business where both essential and unessential tasks are consuming too much time, and areas where certain tasks could be done more efficiently by different personnel.

ANALYZING ALTERNATIVES AND SELECTING ONE

Among the set of alternative strategies for achieving the firm's goals, the firm's managers must select the strategy that looks best. There are two basic approaches for selecting among alternative strategies: the intuitive approach and the analytic approach. Under the intuitive approach, the manager selects the strategy that feels right, based on the manager's experience and business instincts. Under the analytic approach, the manager attempts to estimate the likely results and risks associated with each alternative and select the one that has the best expected outcome, taking the risks into account. Each approach has its strengths and weaknesses; most successful firms combine the two.

While computerized spreadsheets, or even the backs of envelopes, can provide more than ample opportunities for managers to analyze alternative business strategies, a large assortment of more sophisticated tools is available to managers who wish to augment their intuition with rigorous analysis. These tools resulted from two major developments: the refinement and widespread application of industrial engineering (or operations research) techniques to a variety of military and industrial problems since 1940, and the computer technology explosion that has occurred since the 1960s.

Sophisticated analytic tools are primarily of two types: *optimization* techniques, which solve mathematically for the best solution to a particular quantifiable problem, and *simulation* techniques, which generate a distribution of plausible outcomes for each strategy, usually using a computer, allowing the manager to infer which strategy is best.

Optimization techniques solve for the best allocation of resources over time or across business sectors, giving precise solutions to problems that tend to be somewhat limited in complexity. The most widely used set of optimization techniques employ a mathematical approach known as linear programming for solving such problems as: determining the optimum mix of inputs to maximize output, subject to a budget constraint; determining the latest time when each task and subtask of a project must begin in order to finish the entire project in the least amount of time; and determining the least-cost route for delivering a given amount of product from a number of supply points to a number of demand points.

Simulation techniques provide less mathematically sophisticated solutions to resource allocation problems than do optimization techniques, but they provide solutions to highly complex problems that optimization techniques can't easily address. Examples of problems that lend themselves to simulation techniques include: determining the number of processing stations (such as supermarket checkout stands, toll booths on a bridge, elevators in a building, etc.) needed to ensure that waiting time does not exceed certain limits, under various peak load demand conditions; selecting among alternative plant layouts, production line design and staffing alternatives; and testing alternative technical strategies for a financial institution's buying and selling of securities.

One of the more popular analytic techniques, which combines the unique best solution property of optimization with the ability to describe problems in simulation-level detail, is called decision analysis. This technique consists of laying out each strategy (e.g., to acquire rights to a new product, develop a similar product in-house, or not engage in the new product area at all) and each contingency (competition either arises in that product market during the coming year or it does not) in terms of a decision tree; estimating a probability for each contingency; and then estimating the consequences of each possible combination of strategy and contingency. The strategy chosen is the one that maximizes the manager's expected utility, where utility is a mathematical expression of how the various consequences add up to management satisfaction.

Using elegant analytic tools such as linear programming and decision analysis is not a requirement for financial success. Indeed, these tools can be used to hinder the firm: By setting up arbitrary subjective input values that produce some intended analytic result, a pet strategy can end up receiving the support of an apparently rigorous justification. Such tools are best used to divide and conquer complex problems that severely tax intuitive reasoning. They can support good judgment; they can't replace it.

DEVELOPING A PLAN AND A CORRESPONDING OPERATING BUDGET

To reiterate briefly, the planning process begins with broad generalizations about the business and its goals; then, within that broad context, the various ways of achieving those goals most effectively and efficiently are considered. Having selected a general strategy that appears best, it is now time to crystalize the planning process with specifics—the detailed plan and a corresponding operating budget.

The need for specifics at this point calls for the engagement of everyone in the organization who will be responsible for carrying out the plan. As a rule, those who are most intimately familiar with the particulars of task are best equipped to develop the detailed plan for that task. Failure to involve those who must execute the tasks in the development of detailed plans is doubly dangerous: It often produces uninformed plans, and it tends to alienate those who execute from those who plan. Some aspects of a plan can simply be too complex to entrust to any single person, regardless of his or her position on the organization chart.

How does the responsibility for developing the detailed plan get delegated? It generally starts at the top with the chief executive officer's statement of companywide goals and targets, and divides along the firm's functional lines. Even in fairly small firms, one person usually has responsibility for the production of goods or the delivery of services, and another person for marketing.

EXHIBIT 8-5
Revenue Projections by Profit Center and Sales Person
Fictitious Computer Store, Inc.
January 19XX

	Sales Person			
Product Line	Smith	Jones	Brown	Total
Computers	$100,000	$50,000	$10,000	$160,000
Printers	50,000	25,000	5,000	80,000
Other hardware	50,000	25,000	5,000	80,000
Supplies	10,000	5,000	1,000	16,000
Software	5,000	50,000	5,000	60,000
Maintenance contracts	5,000	5,000	25,000	35,000
Service fees	1,000	1,000	75,000	77,000
Total	$221,000	$161,000	$126,000	$508,000

The chief executive officer might, for example, ask the head of production to make the following modifications to last year's detailed plan: redesign the assembly process so that output will be increased by 25 percent by the end of the year at the lowest cost; introduce robotics on a trial basis in one phase of production; and upgrade a particular product so that it outperforms the major competing product in a certain way. The head of marketing might be asked to develop the following: monthly sales targets for each salesperson, by product and service line (see Exhibit 8-5 for an example of a computer store); a plan for achieving those targets; a pricing plan for the product that the production department is upgrading; a new discount price structure for volume purchases and cash transactions; a more aggressive commission rate and smaller base salary option for the sales staff; and an ad campaign for a new product or service line the firm will soon acquire.

Similar planning responsibilities might be delegated in the areas of finance and accounting (e.g., develop a plan to convert the old accounting system to a new computer system that has become the industry standard—see Exhibit 8-6); customer services (develop a plan to improve our service manuals and

EXHIBIT 8-6
Plan to Modernize the Firm's Accounting System

Task	1	2	3	4	5	6	7	8	9	10	11	12
						Month						
1. Review prospective systems (Ames)	- - - -											
2. Purchase best system (Ames)		-										
3. Set up general ledger module (Lee)			- - - - - -									
4. Set up payables and receivables (Lee)				- - - - - -								
5. Set up payroll module (Johnson)						- - - - - -						
6. Set up inventory module (McCoy)						- - - - - -						
7. Validate against old system (All)						- -						

manage a hotline 12 hours each weekday) and research and development (develop two specific alternative product redesign models that fix a frequent customer complaint about our leading product, test both alternatives, and work with marketing to select one and with production to implement it).

In larger firms, the plan will be more elaborate, built up within each division by those who are most familiar with the details. In smaller firms, the plan is generally less complex, often developed by one or two people.

Regardless of the size of the firm, the plan is developed by task, with each task clearly described, the person responsible for each task clearly identified, and planned completion dates explicitly set.

No business plan is complete without an operating budget. The *operating budget* expresses the results of the plan in detail: projections of revenues, costs, and profits by profit center or center of responsibility; the general ledger account balances that are expected to follow; and cash flow requirements and balances throughout the planning period.

Firms commonly create a 12-month budget at the start of the fiscal year. Many revise that budget each month and add a month at the end, thus maintaining a continuous 12-month revolving budget projection. While the continuous budget involves more work, it also tends to induce managers to be more conscious about the future throughout the year.

Let's take the case of the computer store of Exhibit 8-5 to see how an operating budget can be created. Suppose the revenue projections shown represent a 20 percent increase in total revenue, with larger percentage increases projected in software sales, system maintenance contracts, and service fees than in hardware sales. By making reasonable assumptions about gross profit margins as a percent of sales by product line, based on industry trends (e.g., if the industry-wide margin in hardware declined from 27 percent to 25 percent last year, one might assume that it will continue to decline from 25 percent to 23 percent this year), estimates of the costs of goods sold by product and service line should be fairly straightforward.

Estimates of operating expenses should be equally straightforward (say that they increased by five percent last year and can be expected to increase by seven percent this year, taking into account the costs of converting the company's accounting system). The timing of costs and revenues should be built in to the projections, based on the company's experience of seasonality and the schedule of its accounting system conversion project. These estimates permit the company to create a *pro forma* (projected) income statement, from which cash balances and external financing needs can be estimated and expressed in a pro forma balance sheet. From these details, a precise operating budget can be constructed, structured along the lines of the firm's income statement and incorporating its cash flow projections. The detailed steps in building the pro forma income

EXHIBIT 8-7
Building Pro Forma Financial Statements

I. *Pro Forma Income Statement*

1. Estimate revenues based on the firm's recent historical trend in revenues, adjusted for divergences from the trend based on the firm's marketing plan and assumptions about the competition, economy, and other pertinent factors.
2. Estimate cost of sales as a percent of revenues, based on the firm's historical trend and adjusted for the plan.
3. Estimate operating expenses (OE) based on the plan and trends in both absolute OE levels and OE as a percent of revenue.
4. Estimate taxes and calculate the forecast of after-tax profit.

II. *Pro Forma Balance Sheet*

1. Add estimated profit to retained earnings to yield estimate of capital at year end.
2. Determine acquisitions, enhancements, and sale of fixed assets based on the net rate of return estimates associated with each major asset.
3. Estimate inventory, accounts receivable, and accounts payable as percentages of revenues based on the firm's plan and its recent trends.
4. Estimate cash balances before external financing.
5. Calculate external financing needs and revise cash balances.

---

statement and balance sheet needed to create the firm's operating budget are shown in Exhibit 8-7.

Creating an operating budget for a more complex or dynamic setting is more involved, but the essential principles are the same. By integrating the projections of each detailed segment of the business in this way, the firm's needs can be determined and expected financial results can be projected in the aggregate with greater accuracy.

The budget projections almost never turn out to be precisely accurate. Some developments that profoundly affect the bottom line are difficult, if not impossible, to predict. A large corporation's revenues may go flat because of an unexpected organized labor problem. The small firm can incur large and unbudgeted legal expenses if it is sued by a customer or former employee regarding some freak matter.

EXHIBIT 8-8
Why Budget?

1. To make the plan more explicit by quantifying it in terms of dollars.
2. To provide a clearer, more informed basis for negotiation and decision making within the organization.
3. To bring closure to issues involving the importance of competing organizational needs—by product or service line; division, department, or branch; type of labor, type of plant and equipment; future (e.g., R&D) or current (e.g., inventory)—in tangible dollar terms.
4. To create limits on spending authority.
5. To provide a standard—a specific target amount—against which actual values can be assessed.
6. To provide an historical record of the ability of management to predict and control costs.

If the process is so involved and often very inaccurate, why bother budgeting? The operating budget does much more than assist the firm in determining its financial needs and estimating important financial aggregates. In developing a plan for achieving the firm's profit, compensation, and other financial goals and making it dollar-specific for each profit center and task, the operating budget makes the firm's course and its priorities explicit. It induces management to figure out specifically how to achieve a target level of profit and other financial goals. It gives the firm's managers a tangible basis for managing and other employees a lucid context for doing what they do. It moves the plan from the abstract to the real and thus gives it vitality. The operating budget, in short, brings commitment to the planning process. (See Exhibit 8-8.)

The operating budget also gives top management one more timely opportunity to modify the plan before it gets implemented. Many a plan that seemed terrific before its dollar implications were spelled out have been brought down to earth by the operating budget. The insight that a thoughtful budget thus provides can significantly enhance the prospect of profitability—and save the firm from financial ruin.

DEVELOPING CONTROL AND ADJUSTMENT PROCEDURES

Plans without effective controls are akin to laws without effective sanctions. A pleasant concept, maybe, but not very practical. What do we mean by effective controls? Ones that have four characteristics:

1. The results are measurable and closely monitored, with the plan and operating budget used as the monitoring standard;

2. Those responsible for meeting goals and budget amounts are held accountable for the actual results;

3. Deviations from the plan are evaluated so that corrective action can be taken on a timely basis; and

4. The plan has some flexibility, so that procedures exist for modifying the firm's course when the results depart significantly from the plans.

While planning and control are widely thought of as distinct, complementary processes, they are in fact closely intertwined. An effective plan establishes its own control mechanisms, and effective controls generally include provisions for the modification of the plans.

Controls can be critical for providing an early warning system for problems as they occur at their source. Detailed plans and targets generally provide such early feedback to keep minor problems from becoming catastrophes. Effective quality control procedures, for example, turn up production problems long before the products leave the production line and result in returned goods and customer complaints. Such procedures often focus on the production process itself, together with random inspection of goods as they come off the production line, rather than random inspection alone. Weekly staff meetings serve as another useful control vehicle in many organizations to ensure that short-term plans and targets are on course and that problems are nipped in the bud.

One of the challenges in setting up the firm's control mechanisms is to establish a proper balance between ambitious targets and the control mechanisms that are put in place to ensure strict accountability. Managers often experience tension between the two. Ambitious targets can be an effective motivator, but targets that are too ambitious are less likely to be achieved, regardless of control mechanisms. And control mechanisms that punish those who fail to meet revenue, production, or cost control targets are likely to cause the planner not to commit to ambitious but achievable targets. Experience usually tells how ambitious the targets should be, and how onerous the control mechanisms should be.

Responsible people can generally be counted on to create both ambitious plans and their own effective control mechanisms to ensure accountability. They may fall short of their goals in some areas, but given the latitude to fail in some areas and succeed in others, they can usually be counted on to succeed in reaching ambitious overall targets.

Even responsible people, however, often fall short of their targets, both in individual areas and overall. What then? Well, it's usually a good idea to examine the reasons for failure to meet targets. In many instances, it turns out that the plans were simply not sound to begin with. They may have been based on an unanticipated development ("We had no idea the union would go on strike"), or they may have assumed that something would happen that didn't ("We had no idea that our government contract would not be renewed because of fiscal cutbacks").

Whatever the explanation, and regardless of whether it really could have been anticipated, it's useful to examine how those developments are likely to affect other parts of the business as well, if at all. If the implications are serious, it may be necessary to overhaul the plan and the operating budget. Doing so can cut losses and put the firm back on a winning course.

Suppose our manager misses the next round of targets as well? If we're not placing unreasonable pressures on the manager at the planning stage, we may have to question whether this manager is really right for the job at this time. A recurring pattern of unmet goals often suggests either one who hasn't learned to plan, or one who hasn't learned to execute, or both.

OBTAINING COMMITMENTS

Unmet goals are not always the result of management skills not yet learned. Managers who have already proven themselves sometimes fail to rise to the occasion. Why? Perhaps the most basic cause of failure to set ambitious targets and execute plans that produce the desired results is lack of commitment. Without commitment, plans are little more than pipe dreams.

Commitment stimulates focus, clarity of purpose, and discipline, and these qualities cause plans to get executed naturally, if not effortlessly. (Commitment need not imply effort; 80-hour weeks can be effortless for a committed workaholic. The greatest effort for such people is typically in going home after a 14-hour day.) With commitment, even managers lacking in experience make it their business to either quickly learn what they need to know or find someone they can rely on to fill critical knowledge gaps in order to get their jobs done.

Some people seem to be more naturally committed to setting ambitious goals and then attaining them than others. Appearances, however, often mislead. When you can't find naturally committed people, you have no choice but to convert the ones who are available into committed people. People who don't seem to be naturally committed are usually committed people just waiting for a little inspiration.

Creating commitment, and maintaining it where it already exits, is the hallmark of leadership. Commitment is contagious, and a committed leader stimulates others to be committed as well.

Stimulating commitment to producing results, of course, isn't exactly the same as obtaining commitments to a formal plan. We tend to think of those who stimulate commitment as leaders, and those who ask us to sign formal statements of commitment as bureaucrats. In fact, obtaining specific commitments goes hand-in-hand with stimulating commitment. When we're really committed, we're generally more than willing to state it as a matter of record. The formal statement, in turn, clarifies and validates our commitment and serves as a reminder to remain committed. Effective leaders generally stimulate commitment by stating, for the record, their own commitments to the plan, and obtaining similar commitments from others.

EXECUTING THE PLAN: WORKING SMART VS. WORKING HARD

Executing the plan is usually the most time-consuming phase of the planning process, but not necessarily the most difficult. When the plan has been developed with commitment and intelligence, execution tends to be straightforward, like driving the car along a known route. Execution tends to be more difficult when the plan has been developed as a necessary evil or uninformed exercise—when the route has not been thoughtfully laid out in advance.

Most effective executives know that working smart usually produces better results than working hard, if they can't have both. Working smart can mean little more than following the basic steps of good planning and control procedures: getting clear about goals, identifying an efficient course for achiev-

EXHIBIT 8-9
Basics of Planning and Control: A Summary

Step	Objective
1. Define the business, state goals and assumptions.	Lay the foundation for effective planning and control by getting clear about the basics of the firm.
2. Develop a strategic plan.	Establish a basic strategy in the light of the firm's external environment.
3. Develop the baseline forecast.	Project business performance assuming business as usual.
4. Identify alternative business strategies.	Create alternatives that are more profitable than business as usual.
5. Analyze alternatives and select one.	Establish which strategy is likely to be the most profitable.
6. Develop a plan and a corresponding operating budget.	Work out the details of how to execute the most profitable strategy, and make precise estimates of revenues and costs.
7. Develop control and adjustment procedures.	Establish procedures for ensuring that the plan is executed effectively, and how to respond to unforeseen problems.
8. Obtain commitments.	Establish full support and agreements from all persons responsible for plan.
9. Execute.	Do what you said you would do, and support others to do the same.

ing them, developing plans and budgets that make the firm's course explicit, putting effective controls and adjustment procedures in place, and obtaining commitments so that those who execute the plan can do so without feeling victimized by it.

Executing the plan amounts to working smart when the planning process that precedes it has been done with commitment and thoughtfulness. Executives whose firms are consistently profitable generally settle for nothing less than that.

9

PRICING FOR PROFIT

. . . cost of production has very little to do with price at any given time, after the goods have been produced or their production irrevocably determined upon. The relation of cost to price is always that of setting a standard toward which price will tend in the future to conform, and of course it is expected future costs and not actual present or past costs which do even this.

—FRANK H. KNIGHT

One of the tough decisions facing most businesses is how to price goods and services. If the price of a good or service is too high, revenues will be lost excessively as customers turn to competitors. If the price is too low, revenues could be insufficient to cover costs even if the sales volume is high. Where is the happy medium?

THE PROFIT RANGE: THE IMPORTANCE OF OUR COSTS AND THEIR PRICES

The happy medium lives within the *profit range*, a range of prices where the firm at least breaks even in producing and delivering a good or service. (See Exhibit 9-1.) The low end of

127

EXHIBIT 9-1
The Price-Profit Relationship

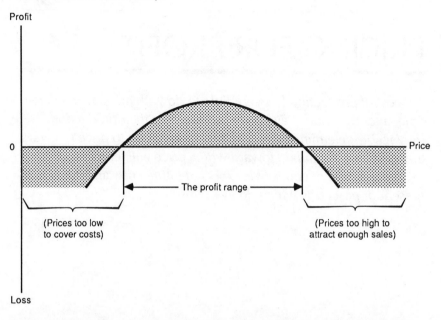

the profit range is the price at which the firm just covers its costs of producing the good or service. Unless the firm is in-efficient in its production or marketing of the good or service sold, this price will usually beat the prices that competitors are charging; but that doesn't make it a good price to charge. The upper end of the profit range is the price at which customers are lost to competitors because their prices are sufficiently lower—lost to such an extent that the reduced volume of sales has lowered revenues right down to the level of the costs of producing the good or service.

The best price, the price that maximizes profit, is somewhere between those limits. A price that is slightly above the low end of the profit range will generally produce revenues that exceed costs, as will a price that is slightly below the high end of the range. As the firm moves its price away from either limit to-ward the other end of the profit range, the rate at which additional (not total) revenues exceed additional costs will decline, up (or down) to the price at which additional revenues are equal to additional costs. At that price, profits are maximized.

SUPPLY AND DEMAND SIMPLIFIED

The proposition that profit is maximized by setting the price at a level that causes additional revenues to equal additional costs—a proposition that can be proven mathematically—comes primarily from a branch of economics known as microeconomic theory, not from the business world. The reader interested in the specifics of this theory should consult a good economics textbook. The proposition is limited in that the information needed to find the profit maximizing price is rarely available. A few aspects of the theory are nonetheless useful to, and understood in a practical way by many of, those who must set prices. One widely understood principle is that market prices tend to be in the vicinity of the intersection of the demand and supply curves. (See Exhibit 9-2.) Let's take a look at those curves.

The Demand Curve

Consumers usually buy less of a good or service as its price goes up. They turn to substitute goods and services, or they just do without. In the parlance of economics, demand curves slope downward. Commercial and household budgets, after all, are limited, and people normally try to get as much profit or value as they can from the dollars they have to spend, so they make it their business to watch the prices of the things they buy.

The important question for most price-setting decisions has

EXHIBIT 9-2
Supply and Demand Curves

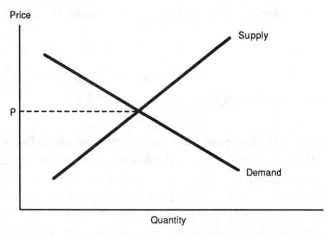

to do with the *slope* of the demand curve: If we raise (or lower) our price by, say, 10 percent, how many fewer (more) units will we sell? The question is important because the total revenue from the sale of any good or service is equal to the price of the item times the number of units sold. If, at any particular margin, a 10 percent change in the price produces more than a 10 percent change in the quantity sold, a price increase will increase revenue; if it produces less than a 10 percent change in the quantity sold, revenue will decline at that margin. (We say, "at a particular margin" because the effect of a change in price on the quantity sold generally differs at different points along the curve.)

When the slope of the demand curve is steep, a change in the price of the good will have less impact on the number of units sold than when the slope is gentle; economists refer to this as an inelastic demand curve. This condition exists when there are no good substitutes for the good or service, and when the customers are not inclined to do without it. Examples are plentiful: the price of gas at the only gas station for miles around, the price of a speeding ticket, the hourly rate of the most expensive psychiatrist in Beverly Hills, the price of a painting by Vermeer, and so on.

When customers can turn to good substitutes for a particular product or service, or when they can easily do without the item and its substitutes, the demand curve will have a gentle slope, and a small change in the price of a good or service charged by a particular seller will have a large impact on the quantity sold by that seller. Examples include the price of basic commodities, (e.g., paper, steel, and wheat) and the price of a share of common stock of any Fortune 500 company.

The sensitivity of the quantity sold to the price charged for the goods and services of most businesses tends to be somewhere between those two extreme sets of examples. Even when, in the short run, a firm can expect a 10 percent increase in price to bring about less than a 10 percent reduction in the quantity sold, it will often be inclined not to increase its price because of the longer term harmful impact it might reasonably expect such a price increase to have, by attracting competition.

The Supply Curve

If the demand curve describes the willingness of consumers to purchase a particular good or service at different prices, the supply curve describes the willingness of producers to make the good or service available at different prices. As the price of the item goes up, producers will be attracted away from less profitable ventures into the production of this item: supply curves slope upward.

The slope of the supply curve, like that of the demand curve, should influence the pricing decisions of individual firms in the market. The slope reflects the rate at which price increases will induce other firms to leave less profitable markets to enter this one. The steeper the slope of the supply curve, the quicker others will be inclined to enter the market.

Suppose good X becomes very popular, and its price gets bid

up as a result. If firms can shift labor and other resources from other enterprises to the production of good X, and if the price increase can be expected to stick for a period of time long enough to justify the resource shift, they'll make the shift. Some examples of such markets from the 1980s are: liability insurance, the services of lawyers who specialize in mergers and acquisitions, and premium beer made by microbreweries.

Managers who must set prices in such markets don't always consult an economist or even think about a supply curve. Before changing prices, however, they do tend to think about the primary factors that shape the curve: the expertise and other inputs that are needed to compete in this market, and the length of time it will take for the competition to obtain those inputs.

PRICING BASED ON COSTS

Even though the pricing decision rarely involves sophisticated economic analysis, it is nonetheless usually based on the factors that influence supply and demand curves—especially the costs of producing and delivering the good or service, on the supply side, and the prevailing prices of similar goods or services and the extent to which a change in price will affect the number of units sold, on the demand side.

One of the simplest ways to set prices is to focus primarily on the supply side: Set prices by adding a markup to the costs of producing and delivering the good or service. What markup? It could be a standard percentage of costs, or it could be a reasonable markup based on costs plus a target profit.

As a practical matter, the relationship between a firm's costs and the selling price it selects for a particular good or service depends on a variety of factors. It depends on the product and the industry; when data on costs are not sound in a particular market, for example, the selling price might be only loosely related to costs. It depends also on the interests of the owners of the firm; prices might be less closely related to costs, for example, when the producers of a new product are more interested in short-term profits than in long-term profits. And the margin between prices and costs depends on prevailing business conditions; the margin might decline, for example, when labor market conditions change such that turnover increases in the marketplace—the firm may wish to give up some profits in order to pay more to its employees so that it can avoid the costs, both recorded and hidden, associated with higher labor turnover.

The relationship depends also on whether the firm uses recent actual or anticipated future costs as the basis on which to calculate the markup, and the assumption the firm's managers make about excess capacity in calculating costs. If its costs are expected to rise and they don't, or if operation at full capacity is assumed and excess capacity prevails, the managers could price the firm out of its markets; if the opposite were to hold true, the firm could price its goods too low to create enough gross profits to cover its fixed costs.

Justification for Cost-Based Pricing: Reduced Uncertainty

Perhaps the most compelling reason to use a cost-based rather than demand-side pricing approach is that it reduces uncertainty. The most significant area of uncertainty that most entrepreneurs face has to do with revenues—costs tend to be much more predictable. Using standard markup approaches is simple, and it avoids expensive market research to obtain, at best, imperfect information about demand, but it does much more. Raising prices (or lowering them) based on changes in costs rather than on demand-side considerations minimizes the risk that the price rise (decline) will significantly disrupt the firm's sales volume.

Sometimes competitors' prices shift for reasons other than

changes in costs—for example, because new firms enter or leave the market, or because consumers' tastes or disposable incomes change. In such cases, the firm may wish to change its standard markup in order to reduce uncertainty about losing sales.

Why is uncertainty about sales volume such a problem? Because few firms have a really good idea about the trade-off between the number of units of a good or service sold and the profit margin or markup on each unit sold. The firm can create serious problems for itself if it doesn't have a good idea about the extent to which a change in the markup, say from 10 percent to 15 percent, will affect the volume of sales. Even small errors in attempts to make such estimates can be very costly.

The prospect that raising prices will induce some unknown portion of the firm's customer base to turn to the competition, or that lowering them will bring in a level of business that the firm can't handle, is bad enough. For many businesses, however, it doesn't take much of a change in the number of units sold to substantially unsettle the firm's operations.

In the case of a price rise and a concomitant reduction in business, excess capacity is expensive, but having to let employees go, trying to sublet space, and finding other ways to rid the firm of excess capacity can be not only expensive, but extremely unpleasant as well. To make matters worse, there's no guarantee that the price increase will offset this decline in business, even ignoring those additional costs. A small increase in price is capable of producing a large decline in the number of units sold.

If a small price increase can bring about a disproportionate decline in business, so can a small price reduction bring about a disruptive increase in business. Customer orders that exceed the firm's productive capacity typically result, at least in the short term, in delays in delivery and a decline in the quality of the good or service, excessive overtime expenses, morale problems for employees who get spread too thin, and expansion costs, which often create tomorrow's excess capacity. What is worse, these disruptions frequently cause loss of goodwill among customers, which defeats the purpose of the price reduction as a demand-side strategy in the first place.

Seasonal and random variation in demand is quite enough for most managers to have to contend with; to add another, potentially more volatile, element of uncertainty looks like insanity to many otherwise risk-taking executives.

Historical Costs and Replacement Costs

For any given markup of price over cost, errors in estimating future costs are likely to reduce profits. The use of actually incurred historical costs, while valid for financial accounting purposes, can create an even larger reduction in profits. Why? Because historical costs, while required for financial accounting purposes, are not the costs that are actually incurred when the current inventory must be replenished. When inventory replacement costs are higher than the historical costs, prices based on costs will be too low; when the costs decline, they will be too high.

The relevant cost for managers interested in finding the profit-maximizing price for a particular good or service is the cost of replacing each item needed to bring the good or service to the customer, regardless of what the item actually cost the firm when it was purchased. A jeweler who purchased gold for less than $100 per ounce in 1960 would obviously be foolish to price the same gold 25 or 30 years later using a markup based on the 1960 price.

It is equally foolish to set prices based on historical costs when the costs have declined. Suppose, for example, that a computer store owner attempted to sell a batch of outdated computers for a price based on what the store paid for the computers after their cost had dropped substantially. The store will surely sell the computers at a loss at a price based on the lower replacement cost of the computers, but it would sustain an even *greater* loss if it attempted to sell them at a price based on the original cost. Customers would exercise very poor judgment to buy any at all at such a price.

If the book values of a firm's inventory and other assets are a distortion for the purpose of assessing the worth of the company, they are disastrous for the purpose of pricing the firm's goods and services. For pricing purposes, the real costs of jewelry and computers—and every other good or service—are the costs of replacing them.

Case of Highly Competitive Markets

Some markets, such as those that farmers and stockbrokers typically deal in, operate on extremely small margins between costs and prices. In such markets the seller sells at prevailing market prices and attempts to overcome small unit profit margins with large volume. As the costs of producing go up or down in these markets, so do prices.

Pricing is pretty easy in this environment. If the firm's prices are set above the market, the sales volume will decline to a level such that the firm's gross profits will probably not cover its operating expenses. If its prices are set below the market, the firm will probably not have a positive gross profit in the first place. In the case of highly competitive markets, the firm's prices are generally set at the market.

Case of Monopolistic Competition

Most goods and services are sold under conditions that amount to less than perfect competition: Competing goods and services are rarely identical to those of a particular firm; the information about the competing goods and services is usually less than perfect; and the consumer typically faces costs of searching for a better deal elsewhere that exceed the expected saving of the potentially better deal. As a result, most firms can exercise some discretion over the amount of their markup.

Obviously, this does not mean that firms can set prices however high they like when the competition is less than perfect. The higher the markup, the greater the incentive for the consumer to search for an alternative, and the greater the incentive for competitors to move in to the territory. Monopolies are usually local and temporary; over a long time horizon, most markets are essentially competitive.

Full Cost vs. Incremental Cost Pricing

If prices are to be based on costs, the firm's managers must answer the question, "Which costs?" Firms that set prices based on costs generally use either of two alternatives: *full cost pricing* or *incremental cost pricing*. Both methods of pricing include the variable or direct cost of producing and delivering the good or service, plus a profit.

The difference between the two methods has to do with the way overhead costs are handled. Under full cost (or absorption) pricing, all of the firm's overhead costs are apportioned into the price of the good or service. Under incremental (or direct) cost pricing, only direct costs and those indirect costs that are closely attributable to the good or service produced (variable overhead costs) are included in the price.

The full cost system is required for external reporting purposes. The incremental cost system is used primarily for management purposes; it is not acceptable for external reporting.

Perhaps the most important difference between these two cost-based pricing systems is this: The costs of excess capacity are recovered explicitly under full cost pricing; they are not under incremental cost pricing. As a result, full cost pricing generally means higher prices and, in the short run, more excess capacity than incremental cost pricing. Because lower selling prices generally result in more units sold, incremental cost pricing is capable of using up excess capacity and yielding more revenue than full cost pricing, even at the lower prices.

More revenue, however, does not necessarily mean more profit. The risk of using incremental costs as the basis for pricing is that the lower prices associated with this system may reduce the profit margin on each unit sold to a level such that, even at the higher volume, gross profits no longer cover operating expenses. Hence, incremental cost pricing is not usually a prudent long-term pricing strategy.

Incremental costs may be a useful basis for allocating costs to profit centers for internal management purposes, but for pricing purposes they tend to be most profitably used only when excess capacity becomes a serious short-term problem. This is especially common when demand is seasonal; tourists expect to pay more for a Caribbean vacation in the winter than in the summer even though overhead costs remain constant throughout the year. It is tempting also to use an incremental cost pricing system when the firm's services or finished goods are not moving at full cost prices. Such a price reduction is likely to be effective, however, only if it is the exception rather than the rule; it can be disastrous if used for an extended period, except when costs are declining over the period, since the use of incremental cost pricing over the long haul means that revenues will not cover the firm's indirect costs.

Even in those circumstances when the firm does not use full costs as the basis for its prices, knowing them can provide useful information in negotiations with important customers.

Cost-Based Pricing and the Robinson-Patman Act

In 1936 President Franklin Roosevelt signed the Robinson-Patman Act into law, thus making it illegal to charge two different prices for a given good or service (the practice of price discrimination) to two different customers in such a way that lessens competition. The best defense against an alleged violation of this law is a rigorous analysis (ideally done before the respective prices were set) demonstrating that the full costs of serving one of the customers were higher than the full costs of serving the other.

PRICING BASED ON DEMAND

In many instances, pricing is primarily a matter of demand-side rather than cost considerations. In some industries, such as textiles, shoes, and computer software, information about actual production costs has not traditionally been as sound as in the steel, auto, computer hardware, and other industries that have depended on more rigorous cost accounting procedures. When reliable cost data are not available, it becomes necessary to rely more on prevailing prices and demand-side considerations as the bases for setting prices.

Case of Established Competition

When the product or service and its competition have been on the market for a while, there is usually less room for discretion in pricing. In such circumstances the firm will be more inclined to accept the prevailing price and try to increase its market share through advertising, superior service, and product differentiation—finding market niches where the competition is less intense.

If it can bring the good or service to the market at the prevailing price but do so at a lower cost than the competition, the firm will generate more profit than its competitors. This profit can, in turn, be used to satisfy a variety of needs: to develop new products or services, purchase modern equipment for the plant and thus lower costs further, for still more advertising, or it can be distributed to the owners and employees. Because of the enormous advantage that such cost efficiency can bring, many firms make it their business to stay current on the latest production technology and to use professional buyers, brokers, or purchasing agents to buy their raw material.

Case of the New Product or Service

When the product is new and the market is, at the moment, less competitive, the firm can exercise more discretion in setting the price. It can set the price based on cost or it can set the price based more on factors pertaining to the demand side of the market.

Most firms take advantage of the downward slope of the demand curve by setting the price of a new product based on a higher than normal markup. This practice is often referred to as skimming the cream, or simply, *skimming*. They do so precisely because the item is new and the competition has not yet responded. As competition arises, the price can always be lowered. Prices are, after all, generally more flexible downward than upward.

For the individual firm, the disadvantage to skimming is that it encourages competition. In an attempt to discourage competition, many firms use an alternative known as *penetration pricing*—the practice of setting a lower price with the hope of achieving market dominance and attaining greater profits over the long run. The strategy behind penetration pricing is that by setting a competitive price at the outset, the firm will give up some profits in the near term as an investment that retards the encroachment of competition and thus produces greater profits over the long term.

The question whether to skim the cream or set penetration prices, or to compromise between the two, thus boils down to an investment decision. When the executives with pricing responsibility can make rough estimates of the profits that will result, say, by month, under each strategy—estimates that may be made more reliable by surveying the market—they can have a basis for determining which approach to use. (The specifics of analyzing such investment alternatives are discussed in the next chapter.)

The primary difference between the pricing of new and established goods or services is that both the cost and demand variables are better known for established goods or services than for new ones.

The estimates of these variables must be made nonetheless. Consistently profitable firms generally base their decisions to add a new product or service line on an estimate of the return on investment in the new line, which calls for projections of both fixed and variable costs of producing and marketing the good or service, and the revenues that can be expected to follow. When those who make the projections of costs and revenues for a new line are held accountable for achieving an actual level of profitability that corresponds closely to the projections, the estimates are less likely to be distorted and the prices can be set with greater assurance that the number of units sold at that price will not produce losses.

BREAKEVEN ANALYSIS

To help the firm set prices and determine production levels that enhance the prospect of profitable operations, many managers use a tool known as *breakeven analysis*. Given information about the firm's fixed and variable costs, breakeven analysis provides a framework for estimating the number of units of a good or service that must be sold at any particular price in order for the firm to at least break even (i.e., to cover its total costs) in the production of the item.

The breakeven point is the price and corresponding level of quantity sold at which total revenues equal the sum of fixed and variable costs. At a given price, if fewer than the breakeven level of production volume is sold, the firm will sell the good or service at a loss; it will profit if more than that are sold (See Exhibit 9–3.)

Suppose, for example, an architecture firm is considering paying a junior architect $15 per hour (including fringes), and incurring $10,000 in office space and other fixed costs to employ the architect full time. If it bills the time of the junior architect to clients at the rate of $25 per hour—a $10 profit margin per hour billed—it takes 1000 billable hours before it recovers the $10,000 of fixed costs to break even; it loses money on the junior architect if he or she bills less than 1000 hours. If the firm can bill 2000 hours of his or her time to clients, the total revenue from the architect will be $50,000, and the total costs will be $40,000, in which case the firm will clear $10,000 from hiring the person.

Or it can consider billing the new architect's time at a higher rate—say, $30 per hour. Here the breakeven point would

EXHIBIT 9-3
Analysis of Breakeven Production Levels

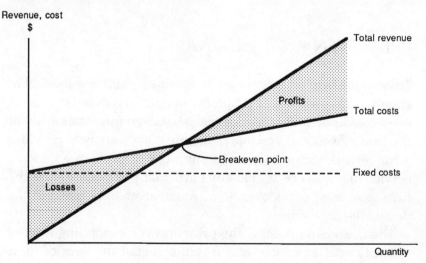

be only 667 hours, and 2000 hours of billed time would yield $60,000 of reveneue, or $20,000 of profit. Of course, the firm may not be able to bill out as much of the junior architect's time at the higher rate, since clients might prefer more of the time of a senior partner when the price of the junior architect goes up.

Breakeven analysis can be extremely useful, but, as the example of the junior architect suggests, it does not address the degree to which the number of units sold will decline as the price of a good or service goes up.

TRANSFER PRICING

Many firms have divisions that sell goods or services to one another. This is standard fare in firms that have organized themselves precisely in order to profit from the economies of vertical integration, the practice of a firm's producing its own raw materials or services at a lower cost than it would otherwise have to bear if it paid for them in the open market. The elimination of advertising is a prominent example of how costs can be reduced under vertical integration without diminishing the quality of the product or service.

When a firm can profit from such economies, it introduces a puzzle to the firm: At what price should one division sell the good or service to the other? In purchasing the needed good or service at a below-market price, the firm creates a buying division that profits from the transaction, but a selling division that sells at a lower markup than competing suppliers. The firm as a whole may profit from the transaction, but the selling division, as a profit center, does not get to show as large a profit as it might otherwise because it is sacrificing those profits for the good of the larger business entity. This poses an obvious problem for the selling division when its managers are compensated on the basis of the profits of the division.

For the company as a whole, the problem is to find a compromise price that balances the inherent advantage to the buying division in a properly functioning vertically integrated firm with the advantage to the selling division in having a captive client and serving a larger corporate purpose. If the two divisions can't agree on such a price, top management must do so for them.

The problem is generally even more complicated than that. Short-term periods of excess capacity in the selling division can induce that division to sell at a loss to the buying division even at or above prevailing market prices. If the buying division were to turn to an outside firm for the purchase during such periods, the selling division could suffer a substantial revenue loss. Top management shouldn't permit such an outside purchase unless the resulting loss to the selling division is smaller than the profit to the buying division—an unlikely condition when the selling entity already has an excess capacity problem.

Outside purchases can, of course, serve the additional purpose of inducing the selling division to stay competitive. Such an inducement may, in some instances, result in more long-term profit for the corporation as a whole than when the buying division continues to feed a chronically inefficient selling division.

In many firms, the selling division operates at full capacity by selling on the open market those goods or services that are not purchased by the buying division. While this might help an outside firm that competes with the buying division, it generally helps the selling firm at least as much by eliminating excess capacity and thus lowering the average cost of production.

The issue boils down to this: The buying division views the price of the good or service as a *variable* cost, while the selling division, and the firm as a whole, bears a *fixed* cost component in the production of the good or service. In a financially secure firm, the buying division can profitably support the selling division by paying higher than market prices during difficult periods of excess capacity, thus absorbing some of the cost of excess capacity that is normal in a world of fluctuating demand, and in return receive bigger price breaks when the selling division is again operating at full capacity. If the excess capacity in the selling division is expected to persist for more than a short period, top management should consider selling that division or liquidating its assets.

Top management would do well, in any case, to set up incentives that lead to a transfer pricing arrangement between divisions of a firm that is mutually advantageous over the long haul, with give-and-take between divisions during swings in market conditions.

PRICING FOR PROFIT: A SUMMARY OF THE ESSENTIALS

The best price is the one that maximizes profits: high enough to yield a profit margin on each unit of good or service sold, but not too high to lose volume to the competition. That price is determined by the supply and demand curves for the firm's goods, and especially by the key factors that shape those curves: on the demand side, the availability of substitute goods and services and the budgets of the prospective buyers; on the supply side, the ease with which prospective competitors can allocate resources away from their less profitable enterprises toward the production of the particular good or service in question.

One of the simplest ways to set prices is to focus primarily on the supply side: Set prices by adding a standard markup to the costs of producing the good or service. That markup should depend on the costs of *replacing* the inventory and other resources needed to bring the product or service to the customer, not the costs that show up on the income statement.

When sound cost data are difficult to obtain, pricing can be based more on demand-side considerations. In the case of an established product or service, the firm usually sets prices at the prevailing market price and tries to increase its market share through advertising and product differentiation. For a new product or service, the firm can either set a high price initially (skimming the cream) and then reduce it as the competition enters, or it can attempt to discourage competition in the first place by setting a lower market penetration price, thus giving up some profits in the short term so that more profits will accrue over the long term.

The pricing decision can often be aided effectively by break-even analysis, a tool for estimating how much profit will result from various prices that might be set for the good or service. While limited by the assumption that the volume sold is insensitive to the price set, breakeven analysis is nonetheless a useful tool for establishing the minimum number of units sold at a given price in order to cover the fixed and variable costs of producing the good or service.

10

ANALYZING INVESTMENT ALTERNATIVES

. . . capital moves toward the best blend of good return and safety that can be found somewhere in the world at any given time.

—WALTER B. WRISTON

Firms make profits by acquiring the right assets and managing them efficiently. Determining what assets to acquire—the investment decision—is the foundation on which the firm's profitability is built.

Deciding what assets to acquire and maintain begins with basic elements of the planning process discussed in Chapter 8: defining the business, stating goals, and identifying alternative strategies for achieving them. Obviously, you can't know what assets to have without first knowing what your business is about and having basic strategies for running it. Each basic business strategy alternative identified as part of the planning process may require a unique set of assets, so the selection among basic strategy options typically calls for the use of tools for projecting and analyzing both the costs of purchasing and maintaining the assets and the likely revenues associated with each option.

Some common examples of basic strategy alternatives that

call for investment decision analysis include the decision to expand an existing product line or develop and promote a new one, and the decision to commit resources to longer term research and development.

Even within a given basic strategy option, the firm usually finds itself having to analyze specific investment alternatives. Once the firm has identified which product and service lines to offer and which specific consumer groups to target, it may find itself having to decide, for example, whether to make or buy various components, or whether to purchase or lease certain resources required to product goods and services for the firm's customers. One variation of the make-or-buy decision is to consider acquiring a supplier; in so doing, the firm will incur additional capital costs in order to make the acquisition, but those costs may be offset by the firm's ability to realize economies associated with the scaling down of the marketing and distribution costs of the acquired entity.

The purchase-or-lease decision involves similar trade-offs. Purchasing the resources involves a commitment of scarce capital for the life of the resources; leasing them usually involves less of a commitment, but leasing is typically more expensive if the resources are kept for any length of time, and leasing deprives the firm of ownership and full freedom to use the resources as the firm's managers desire.

Or the firm may find itself having to decide whether to maintain its existing, possibly outmoded capital facility or equipment, or to incur some capital costs to replace those assets with modern, more efficient counterparts.

The problem of choosing between such alternative commitments of capital, each alternative having different implications for current versus future profits, is the essence of the investment decision. Virtually every firm must face the problem of analyzing investment alternatives and selecting among them. Many firms must do so on a frequent, sometimes daily, basis, outside of a periodic planning process. For investment decisions involving the prospective commitment of significant amounts of capital, or involving comparisons of complex flows of revenues and costs, it makes little sense to make the decision without first assembling the implications of the decision for the firm's short- and long-term profitability.

FUNDAMENTAL ELEMENTS OF INVESTMENT ANALYSIS

Suppose we have identified two investment options and wish to determine which of the two is likely to be the more profitable. The two options may differ in several ways: initial cost outlay; the subsequent stream of costs over the lives of the respective options (the most significant costs tend to be depreciation, maintenance, and salaries); the timing and magnitude of revenues generated by the options; the salvage value of the capital asset at the end of its useful life to the firm; the degree of uncertainty associated with both the cost and revenue streams, and with the estimated salvage value; effects on the profitability of other products and services offered by the firm; tax implications; and effects on the firm' nonfinancial goals.

How does one approach such a thicket of variables? One piece at a time. The analysis begins with a best estimate of the revenue and cost streams of each option. It's generally helpful to graph the revenue and cost projections of each of the options, because we tend to see things more clearly when the data are graphed. An example is given in the tabular date of Exhibit 10-1 and the corresponding graph at Exhibit 10-2. Option A consists of a small engineering firm's continuing its present system of manual drafting with only modest computer support, and Option B involves the firm's purchase of the latest computer-aided design (CAD) hardware and software for each of its engineers. It anticipates operating at a loss during the first

EXHIBIT 10-1
Cost and Revenue Projections for Two Options:
Business as Usual or Invest?

	Option A			Option B		
	($ thousands)			($ thousands)		
Year	Revenues	Costs	Profit	Revenues	Costs	Profit
1	100	50	50	90	100	−10
2	110	55	55	130	105	25
3	120	60	60	180	110	70
4	130	65	65	250	115	135
5	140	70	70	320	120	200

year if it converts to the updated system, because of both higher costs and reduced revenues, with profits for the new system surpassing those associated with the old system by the third year, and substantially higher profits in Years 4 and 5.

ANALYZING PROFIT STREAMS: THE NET PRESENT VALUE, FUTURE VALUE, AND INTERNAL RATE OF RETURN METHODS

Converting the revenue and cost projections to a net profit projection, and then graphing the profit streams for each strategy, frequently reveals one option to be clearly superior to others, so that a decision can be made without further deliberation. Suppose it doesn't? With regard to the illustration of the previous section, the problem at that point boils down to a comparison of the two streams of projected profits: How willing should the firm be to sacrifice a given amount of short-term profit under Option A in order to be able to realize the larger long-term profit associated with Option B?

EXHIBIT 10-2
Comparison of Profit Projections

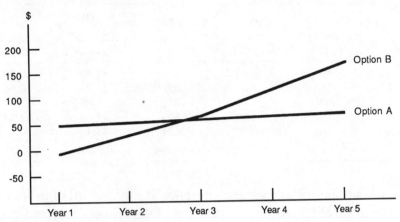

Net Present Value (NPV)

To address this question, we begin by making sure that the projections are as accurate as possible, and then we measure the net present value (NPV) of the profit stream associated with each of the two investments. The NPV of a profit stream is the smallest amount of profit that the firm would just as soon have now in a lump sum as it would to wait for the profit stream in question to materialize. While the present value figure is not one that is actually available to the firm in a lump sum amount, it provides a useful summary index of the worth of a stream of profits, or cash, for analytic purposes. Whichever of the two investment alternatives under consideration generates the profit stream with the larger net present value should be the preferred investment option.

At the heart of the net present value calculation is the notion that we prefer to have any given amount of profit or cash as soon as possible; most of us are willing to have any given amount now rather than wait for a slightly larger amount later. How much more modest for any given time period, or how

EXHIBIT 10-3
Net Present Values of the Profit Streams for Two Options

Year	Option A Profit ($000)	Option B Profit ($000)	10% Discount Factor	Present Values ($000) Option A	Present Values ($000) Option B
1	50	−10	.909	45.45	−9.09
2	55	25	.826	45.45	20.66
3	60	70	.751 •	45.08	52.59
4	65	135	.683	44.40	92.21
5	70	200	.621	43.46	124.18
			Net present values:	223.84	280.55

much sooner for any given difference in the amount of profit or cash to be obtained now rather than later, should depend primarily on three factors: (1) the expected profit streams associated with each of the firm's alternative uses of its capital; (2) the risks associated with those profit expectations and the decision-maker's willingness to incur those risks; and (3) the costs of obtaining more capital to support those alternatives by way of additional debt or equity.

The calculations of the net present values of the profit streams associated with the two options are shown in Exhibit 10-3. They are based on the assumption that the firm's minimum acceptable rate of return—sometimes called the firm's *hurdle rate*—is 10 percent. To simplify the calculations, the profit is assumed to arrive at the end of each year; more precise estimates can be obtained by shortening the projection intervals to months or quarters. Those profits are *discounted* (reduced) to the present by the 10 percent hurdle rate to yield a *present value* profit amount for each year in the projection. (The discount factors can be obtained from standard published financial tables, or from computerized spreadsheet programs, or by calculating them from the formula

$$PV = 1/(1 + r)^n,$$

where PV is the present value of $1 to be earned n years hence, compounded at the hurdle rate r). The total of the discounted profit amounts over all n of the years is the net present value of the profit stream.

For the example at hand, the existing system generates a projected 5-year profit stream that is equivalent to an immediate profit of $223,840, and the new CAD system generates a projected stream equivalent to an immediate profit of $280,550. Assuming that those projections are accurate, the firm should convert to the new system. The firm's hurdle rate would have to be higher than an astronomical 30.1 percent in order for the firm to prefer the old system.

Future Value

Option C for the owners of the firm—occasionally a realistic one, and in any case a useful one to illustrate the basic tools available for analyzing investment alternatives—is to sell the company and invest the proceeds in financial instruments. Suppose the owners could sell the business today for $800,000 and invest that amount in virtually riskless government securities at nine percent. At the end of five years, the *future value* of the sum of the $800,000 principal and the accumulated interest would amount to $1,230,899. [This result can be obtained by finding the future value of a sum of $1 invested at nine percent for five years (1.538624) from a standard financial table and multiplying that amount by $800,000; or by using a modern computerized spreadsheet program with financial functions, such as Lotus 1-2-3®; or by using the formula

$$FV = P(1 + r)^n,$$

where FV is the future amount of the sum, P is the amount of invested principal, r is the interest rate, and n is the number of years of the investment.]

Let's compare this option with Option B. (We can ignore Option A, since we've already established that B is superior.) Under Option B, we start with a business worth $800,000, generate $420,000 of profit over five years (the simple sum of the Option B profits reported in Exhibit 10-3), and end up with a business that is making $200,000 per year and rising. A business with a recent profit trend like that could probably be sold for well over $2,000,000 at that point; that future amount, plus the 5-year accumulation of $420,000 of profit along the way, yields a total future amount of $2,420,000—about twice the future amount of Option C. Based on these estimates, Option C can be rejected.

In simple, nonnumerical language, the owners of the firm in this example can realize substantially more profit by capitalizing on existing opportunities within the business and thus increasing its value than by selling the business before those opportunities are exploited.

Internal Rate of Return (IRR)

When the decision is whether to add to existing operations rather than change them, the analysis is simpler than in the above example; existing operations can usually be left out of the analysis, since, as a rule, they can be assumed not to change much.

Suppose, for example, that our engineering firm can purchase a new facility that will produce a line of instruments that will yield $1000 of profit per unit, and that, starting in a year, the firm can expect to sell 100 instruments per year. Suppose further, that the facility will cost $1 million; that it can be expected to sustain operations for about 20 years before being sold, with an estimated salvage value in the neighborhood of $100,000; that the firm's cost of capital is 10 percent; that it uses the straight-line depreciation method; that the firm is in the 34 percent tax bracket; and that the acquisition would not affect the firm's existing business.

For investments involving large capital commitments up front, the immediate problem usually involves cash rather than profit; it is customary to examine the discounted streams of cash flow rather than profit, where cash flow is normally defined as net profit after taxes plus depreciation. (Cash flow thus defined is equivalent to the firm's net operating income after taxes, before deducting payments to its financial sources.)

In the first year of the investment in the example at hand, the investment will yield a $150,000 pretax loss—$50,000 of depreciation cost (1/20th of $1,000,000) and $100,000 of capital cost (10 percent interest on the unpaid balance of the loan)—a $99,000 net loss after taxes. The first year produces a negative cash flow of $49,000 (negative $99,000 net profit plus $50,000 depreciation); from Years 2 through 20, the operation generates positive and growing cash flow. The entire cash flow stream has a net present value of $277,384. (See Exhibit 10-4.)

A common alternative to the net present value calculation is to find the investment's *internal rate of return* (IRR). This is done by asking, "What would the cost of capital have to be to make the net present value of the cash flow stream equal to zero?" (Stated another way, "At what interest rate would the present value of the $49,000 of negative cash flow in the first year offset the present value of the following 19 years of positive cash flow?") This kind of problem can be solved using brute force trial and error with a calculator and a set of present value tables, but it is most easily solved using a computerized spreadsheet. The answer: 53.9 percent.

If the firm can obtain capital at a rate that is substantially less than the investment's IRR (and if the firm has no better investment opportunities, and especially if the investment looks good in terms of the NPV of the profit stream as well as the IRR of the cash flow stream), the firm should make the investment.

EXHIBIT 10-4
Analysis of the Purchase of a New Facility

Year	Gross Profit	Depreciation	Interest (10%)	Tax (34%)	NPAT	Cash Flow	Discount Factor	Present Value
1	0	50,000	100,000	−51,000	−99,000	−49,000	.9091	−44,545
2	100,000	50,000	95,000	−15,300	−29,700	20,300	.8264	16,777
3	100,000	50,000	90,000	−13,600	−26,400	23,600	.7513	17,731
—	—	—	—	—	—	—	—	—
18	100,000	50,000	15,000	11,900	23,100	73,100	.1799	13,148
19	100,000	50,000	10,000	13,600	26,400	76,400	.1635	12,492
20	200,000	50,000	5,000	49,300	95,700	145,700	.1486	21,657
							Net Present Value of Cash Flow:	$277,384

How much less is substantially less? That depends on the risks that the expected profits of the investment in question will not materialize. Those risks, and how to handle them analytically, are dealt with toward the end of this chapter.

So, net present value and internal rate of return are alternative ways of analyzing investment options. Both collapse cash flow or profit streams into single numbers, based on discounting. The two methods are really quite similar.

When should each be used? With NPV, a hurdle rate is selected as the basis for comparing two or more investment options; an option that is preferred under one hurdle rate might be rejected under a different rate. With IRR, the interest rate is found that makes the NPV of the initial outlay equal to the NPV of the stream of subsequent revenues; whether a risky option with a high IRR is preferred to a less risky option with a lower IRR will depend on the decision-maker's taste for risk. Since the hurdle rate used under the NPV method usually exceeds the firm's cost of capital by a margin that is designed specifically to allow for risks—the same risks that are traded off against different IRR levels—the two approaches should in most cases produce about the same result.

Collapsing Cash Flow Streams: A Recap

Analyzing investments, then, can begin with the process of collapsing a future stream of profit or cash flow back to the present (discounting) based on the net present value (NPV) of the stream (or the internal rate of the return [IRR] variant of the NPV calculation). Or it can begin with the process of calculating the future value of the sum of the principal and interest of the investment (compounding) over some number of equal length time periods.

The key is to ensure that the same method is used to compare any two investment options, and that the time periods used are the same. (Why the same time periods? Because at any

EXHIBIT 10-5
Present Value and Future Value Formulas

Concept	Formula	Definition
Present value	$PV = F/(1 + r)^n$	The current worth of a future amount F discounted over n periods back to the present at interest rate r.
Net present value	$NPV = \overset{n}{\Sigma} PV$	The current worth of a stream of future amounts discounted back to the present.
Internal rate or return	Find r such that $NPV = 0$	The interest rate that sets the PV of the initial outlay equal to the PV of the subsequent stream of profits.
Future value of a sum	$FV = P(1 + r)^n$	The total of principal, P, and accumulated interest over n periods at interest rate r.

given interest rate the returns of a 1-year investment will be less than those of, say, a 5-year investment; to compare the two, an assumption must be made about the rate of return from the firm's reinvesting the proceeds of the 1-year investment at the end of the first year and until the end of the fifth year.) The essential features of each basic method of collapsing profit streams are summarized in Exhibit 10-5.

THE PAYBACK METHOD

Collapsing profit or cash flow projection streams to net present or future values is not the only way to compare investment alternatives. A simpler, and more easily understood, way is to use the *payback method*—how long it takes for the accumulated returns on the investment to match the amount of the initial investment outlay. Other factors held constant, an investment that pays for itself sooner is better than one that does so later.

Other factors, however, are rarely held constant. An investment that pays for itself quickly may run out of steam right afterward, while one that pays for itself a bit later may then blossom forth with a profusion of returns. The payback method has the virtue of simplicity to commend it; beyond that, it is limited. In ignoring the magnitude and timing of returns both before and after the payback point, and in ignoring the cost of capital, this method of evaluating investments effectively ignores the rate of return of the full stream of profits. A firm would generally be extremely shortsighted to rely primarily on the payback method to analyze investment alternatives.

THE LEASE OR BUY DECISION

One common type of investment decision consists of choosing between the purchase or lease of an asset—especially equipment, office space, and land. The primary problem with the purchase option is that it frequently involves a significant commitment of scarce capital up front. With the lease option, there are usually two problems: Leasing typically involves larger costs if the asset is held for any length of time (largely because the lessee is deprived of tax write-offs for depreciation and interest), and it generally restricts the use of the asset in ways that ownership does not (an owned asset can be sold, for example, whereas a leased resource is often more difficult to unload without paying a stiff penalty).

Whether it is more profitable to purchase or lease the asset ordinarily depends on a variety of factors: The purchase price of the asset, the difference between the asset's book value and salvage value at the time of sale, the length of time that the asset is to be used, the terms of the lease, the firm's cost of capital, the firm's marginal tax rate, and risk.

Suppose, for example, that in order to stay competitive, our

EXHIBIT 10-6
Purchase or Lease a Machine?

Purchase Option

Year	Loan Cost (10%)	Depre- ciation	Pretax Cost	Tax Benefit (34%)	After- Tax Cost	Discount Factor (12%)	Present Value of Cost
1	10,000	20,000	30,000	10,200	19,800	0.8929	17,679
2	8,000	20,000	28,000	9,520	18,480	0.7972	14,732
3	6,000	20,000	26,000	8,840	17,160	0.7118	12,214
4	4,000	20,000	24,000	8,160	15,840	0.6355	10,067
5	2,000	20,000	22,000	7,480	14,520	0.5674	8,239
				Net Present Value of Cost:			$62,931

Lease Option

Year	Rental Payment	Tax Benefit (34%)	After- Tax Cost	Discount Factor (12%)	Present Value of Cost
1	30,000	10,200	19,800	0.8929	17,679
2	30,000	10,200	19,800	0.7972	15,784
3	30,000	10,200	19,800	0.7118	14,093
4	30,000	10,200	19,800	0.6355	12,583
5	30,000	10,200	19,800	0.5674	11,235
		Net Present Value of Cost:			$71,375

firm must have a computer with a 5-year productive life, a computer that can either be purchased for $100,000 or leased for $30,000 per year. If we purchase the machine, the bank will lend us the $100,000 at 10 percent. To simplify the calculations, we can assume that the computer will be depreciated on a straight-line basis over its life. Our firm is in the 34 percent tax bracket, and we will build a risk factor into our calculations by using a 12 percent hurdle rate (two percent above our capital cost rate). Do we purchase or lease the computer? The calculations are shown in Exhibit 10-6.

Since revenues should not be affected by the decision, we can leave them out of the analysis. The firm will maximize its profit by choosing whichever option has the cost stream with a lower net present value. Under the purchase option, the after-tax cost of the computer amounts to the annual repayment of principal and interest less the tax benefit associated with the interest and depreciation expenses. Under the lease option, the aftertax cost amounts to the annual rental payment less the taxes associated with that expense. Since the present value of the aftertax cost stream associated with purchasing the computer is less than that associated with the lease of the same equipment, the firm should purchase the machine.

WHICH GAUGE TO WATCH: PROFIT OR CASH FLOW STREAMS?

An investment that has a positive net present value based on its projected cash flow stream may have a negative present value based on its projected profit stream. The example presented in Exhibit 10-4 is a case in point. The NPV and IRR calculations based on cash flows in that example suggest that the firm should invest. The NPV of the projected profit stream of that investment, however, is negative ($-$148,294). The investment produces a large positive cash flow over its 20-year life, assuming the firm will grow and not have to reduce its liabilities by paying off the principal of each loan. If the principal of the loan in this example gets serviced, the cash flow calculations turn out to be the same as the net profit after taxes calculations, since annual depreciation and annual principal repayment are offsetting amounts: $50,000. From a bottom-line *profit* perspective, the investment is not sound.

Cash flow is, of course, extremely important, as was discussed in Chapter 7. Cash flow is, however, primarily a short-term matter. A good investment is one that increases the firm's profits. If it generates cash flow, too, so much the better; over the long term, however, maximizing cash flow streams is useful only to the extent that doing so increases the firm's profits. Remember, the bottom line is at the bottom of the income statement, not at the top of the balance sheet!*

COST OF CAPITAL: DETERMINING THE RIGHT DEBT-TO-EQUITY RATIO

The firm can't invest in profit-producing assets without capital, and capital—like lunch—is rarely free. The total cost of obtaining profit-producing assets usually exceeds the outlay for the assets alone. When the money is raised in the form of new debt, the cost of capital to the firm consists of interest on notes or bonds. When the money is raised in the form of new paid-in equity, such as common stock, the costs consist of dividends, appreciation of the stock (to the degree that that appreciation would have otherwise been captured by the prior base of owners), and the more difficult to measure losses: dilution of corporate control, or use of the owner's personal assets, or both.

For most companies, additional equity (other than retained earnings) is more expensive than additional debt, even ignoring the costs of diluting corporate control associated with new shares of stock. Why? Primarily because interest costs are tax-deductible expenses and dividend payouts are not.

The precise cost of capital to the firm generally depends on whether the existing mix of debt and equity is rich or lean in equity. Banks and other financial institutions usually charge

---

*Some analysts prefer using cash flow streams rather than profit streams, on the grounds that they are simpler—unencumbered by the selection of depreciation methods and accrual assumptions and the discrepancies between reported and "actual" income that are produced by such selections. The profit stream projections used in this chapter, and the streams that managers should use, are based on management's best estimates of actual income streams, not income projected under GAAP.

EXHIBIT 10-7
Determining the Optimal Mix of Debt and Equity

Debt as a % of Total Assets	Debt-to -equity Ratio	After- tax Cost of Debt	Cost of Equity	Weighted Cost
0%	0	4.0%	10%	10.0%
20%	1:4	4.5%	10%	8.9%
40%	2:3	5.0%	11%	8.6%
60%	3:2	6.0%	13%	8.8%
80%	4:1	9.0%	15%	10.2%

lower interest rates to firms that are relatively rich in equity, and the costs of equity tend to be higher than the costs of debt, so firms that are rich in equity can generally minimize capital costs while increasing the risks associated with higher leverage by taking more debt, most often in the form of notes or bonds. Thinly capitalized firms, on the other hand, usually face high interest rates and can generally minimize capital costs—and reduce the risks of bankruptcy and takeover—by raising more equity. The point can be more easily seen with an example— see Exhibit 10-7.

Notice in this example that despite the fact that both the cost of debt and the cost of equity rise as the debt-to-equity ratio increases, the weighted cost of capital declines, and then rises as this firm becomes more highly leveraged. The firm in this example minimizes its capital costs when its total equity is about 50 percent larger than its total liabilities—a debt-to-equity ratio of about 0.67-to-1.

Such a debt-equity mix, while not necessarily optimum for most firms, is not uncommon. The reader will recall, from Chapters 5 and 6 that IBM's debt-to-equity ratio at the end of 1985 was 0.64-to-1, substantially lower than the 1.1-to-1 ratio for the entire computer industry. In 1985, IBM's interest payments were nine percent of its loans (the sum of its average long-term debt and average loans payable during the year), and its dividends per share were three percent of its average common stock price during the year. During that year, the corporation added $8.61 of debt for every dollar of paid-in capital (all from employee and stockholder plans), which seems high given the respective costs of debt and paid-in capital; but it added $5.72 of capital by way of retained earnings for every dollar of debt!

Big Blue provides powerful evidence that by generating its capital mostly through sustained high profits, the firm can reduce its cost of capital in at least three ways: (1) by creating the vast majority of its capital in the form of retained earnings, on which it pays neither dividends nor interest; (2) by giving stockholders a plausible expectation of capital appreciation, so that it can keep its dividends at a modest level and still produce a high return on investment for the stockholders; and (3) by staying so profitable, it also qualifies for bonds with the highest ratings and lowest interest rates.

ASSESSING INVESTMENT RISKS

We have noted that a simple way to incorporate risks into the analysis of investment decisions is to create a hurdle rate that adds a constant risk margin, say from two percent to 10 percent, to the firm's cost of capital in discounting profit or cash flows, with the size of the margin depending on the degree of risk associated with each investment option. While that method is simple, it is also fairly arbitrary. If we think that it's about 50 percent likely that our revenue projections could be too high or too low by a factor of two, does that mean that we should make the hurdle rate two percent higher than the cost of capital? Five percent? Ten percent? Fortunately, there are more precise and less arbitrary methods than that for building risks into the analysis, some of which don't require a great deal of technical sophistication.

One of the simplest methods is to make two or three plausible forecasts of an investment's profit stream—a high and low forecast, each forecast about 50 percent likely; or a high, middle, and low forecast, each about 33 percent likely—and then examine both the expected yield and the spread between the high and low forecasts for each investment option. The more risky an investment, the greater will be that spread. Risk-averse decision-makers tend to prefer investments with less spread.

The spread between the high and low forecasts can, in turn, be analyzed using either sophisticated or fairly simple, less precise methods. The most rigorous methods of incorporating risk into the analysis of investments use not only measurements of the degree of spread between the high and low estimates, but also measurements of the degree of risk aversion of the decision maker. Those variables can be handled using techniques of decision analysis, discussed briefly in Chapter 8. We won't get into that here; for most problems it's just too complicated a method to use, and not always more reliable.

The most straightforward approach is simply to examine each of the forecasts and ask whether the high-end (and, when three scenarios are forecast, the most likely) forecast justifies the risks associated with the low-end forecast. Since the low end forecast has been assumed to be at least 33 percent likely to occur, it must be regarded as a serious risk. This assessment usually can be made by just looking at graphs of each forecast under each investment option.

Let's use the example of Exhibit 10-1 to see how this works. Recall that the problem is whether an engineering firm should continue using its manual design system or whether it should upgrade to a modern computer-aided system. Suppose the firm's managers produce the forecasts shown in Exhibits 10-8 and 10-9.

EXHIBIT 10-8
Building Risks into Profit Forecasts

	Option A			Option B		
	($ thousands)			($ thousands)		
Year	Low	Likely	High	Low	Likely	High
1	45	50	55	−30	−10	10
2	50	55	60	0	25	50
3	50	60	70	40	70	100
4	55	65	75	70	135	200
5	55	70	85	70	200	350

Option A is the current system, so there's less uncertainty in the profit forecast for that option (i.e., less spread around the most likely projection) than for Option B. The issue comes down to whether the managers view the higher profits associated with Option B for the high and middle forecasts as sufficient justification for the risk of lower profits associated with that option for the low forecasts. Since the net present value of the low forecast for Option B ($94,055) is only about $100,000 lower than the NPV of the low forecast for Option A ($191,514),

EXHIBIT 10-9
Graphs of Profit Forecasts That Incorporate Risks

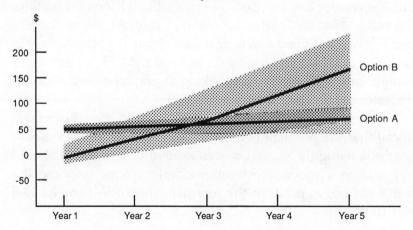

while the NPV of Option B's high-end forecast is nearly $225,000 higher ($479,470 versus $256,183) and the middle forecast is about $55,000 higher, most decision-makers would choose Option B. (This happens to be the same choice as when the risks were ignored, but it often doesn't work out that way. For example, if the low-end forecast for Option B were much lower and the owner of the firm were averse to risk, Option A would be preferred.)

WHAT ABOUT FACTORS THAT ARE DIFFICULT TO MEASURE?

Investment decisions that are based on sophisticated analysis sometimes turn out to be regrettable because the analysis on which the decision was based ignored a difficult-to-quantify, but nonetheless crucial factor. Electric power companies surely would not have invested so heavily in nuclear power plants in the 1970s had the unpopularity of those plants in the communities in which they were built been anticipated and included in the analyses. Nor is it likely that General Motors' purchase of the Ross Perot-controlled Electronic Data Systems Corporation, which looked like a good investment on paper when it was made in 1984, would have been carried out had Ross Perot's outspokenness against GM's executives been anticipated and factored into the analysis.

Investments thus affect revenues and costs in ways that are often virtually impossible to predict and measure. They can affect them by way of harmful, and often helpful, influences on employee morale, community relations, and governmental action.

When they are anticipated but difficult to measure, they can still be factored into the analysis. One way is to estimate their eventual effects on revenues and costs. This approach is limited, however, because it is usually extremely difficult to make such estimates, and because some of these factors may never affect profits.

A simpler, more practical way of handling these factors can overcome the limitations: Simply ask, "How much would we be willing to pay (or receive) now to prevent that problem (benefit) from occurring?" That amount can be factored in as a cost or revenue amount in the initial period, thus giving the qualitative factor a quantitative counterpart that can be dealt with explicitly in the analysis.

ANALYZING INVESTMENT ALTERNATIVES: KEY ISSUES

Some of the most important decisions that confront the firm's managers involve investment alternatives that are too complex to be selected using only intuition. The complexity stems from a host of important factors that are frequently associated with each alternative:

the magnitude and timing of both revenues and costs (taking into account any significant effects on the firm's other goods and services);

depreciation schedules, book values, and salvage values;

the firm's tax bracket;

uncertainty in the forecasts of revenues and costs and the decision maker's willingness to incur the risks associated with those uncertainties; and

the effects of the decision on such intangibles as employee morale and relations with the firm's vendors and customers.

The first step in dealing with such complexity is to forecast the profits under each option. When it's not obvious from the forecasts which option is best, the net present value method of comparing alternative profit streams usually provides the most reliable basis for making a decision.

Three suggestions stand out as especially useful in making those comparisons:

1. focus primarily on the net present value of profits, not on simple but shortsighted criteria such as the payback period;

2. leave out of the analysis all factors that are not affected by the decision (such as revenues in the lease-or-buy decision and profits from existing operations in a decision about whether to acquire an unrelated line of business); and

3. use the same method of analysis to compare the various investment alternatives.

11

IMPROVING THE BOTTOM LINE: THE LARGE CORPORATION

A big corporation is more or less blamed for being big; it is only big because it gives service. If it doesn't give service, it gets small faster than it grew big.

—WILLIAM S. KNUDSEN

The principles of profit making are not just theory. We've referred repeatedly to the behavior of "firms that are consistently profitable"; those are real firms, not hypothetical ones. From a scrutiny of their behavior, and from a scrutiny of the behavior of firms that are not consistently profitable, one can derive a set of principles that constitute a technology of profit making.

A couple of notes of clarification are in order. A *technology* is simply a technical method of achieving a practical purpose; few purposes are more practical than that of profit making. Also, the word technology often connotes something that is sophisticated or complex; that's not intended here. A firm's systematic use of financial data toward the goal of profitability does not have to be either sophisticated or complex in order to be effective.

171

Let's look now at firms that use financial data effectively in the real world toward greater profitability and see what they do, how they do it, and the results they achieve.

AMERICAN BRANDS: PROFITABILITY THROUGH STRATEGIC PLANNING

American Brands, Inc., is a formerly successful company whose star was rising again in the 1980s. Once the largest producer of tobacco products, including Lucky Strike, Pall Mall, Tareyton, and Carlton cigarettes, American launched a major diversification strategy in the mid-1960s. The purpose of that strategy was to reduce its reliance on a product line in which it had been losing ground to its principal competitors, R.J. Reynolds and Philip Morris—a product line, moreover, that health care experts had been pointing to increasingly as a serious public health hazard.

While American, like its larger competitors in the tobacco industry, has steadfastly resisted this escalating attack by a succession of U.S. Surgeon Generals and a brigade of medical researchers, its continuing diversification strategy clearly suggests the company's unease about depending exclusively on a product that has become so controversial.

American's diversification strategy started in 1966 with the acquisition of Sunshine Biscuits, Inc. Twenty years later, American had become one of the world's largest holding companies, with ownership in an array of products that extends beyond tobacco and food to distilled beverages (Jim Beam), office products (Swingline), golf and leisure products (Titleist), personal care products (Jergens), hardware (Master Lock), security (Pinkerton's), and financial and insurance services (Franklin Life and Southland Life). By 1985, American's nontobacco holdings accounted for 40 percent of its sales and 42 percent of its total operating income. ("American" Brands tobacco actually is a bit of a misnomer; the majority of its 1985 tobacco revenues consisted of the sales of tobacco abroad, within the operations of Gallaher Limited, producers of Benson and Hedges and Silk Cut cigarettes.)

Diversification notwithstanding, these numbers indicate that American was still doing a thriving business in tobacco in the mid-1980s. By that time, however, its American Tobacco Company subsidiary had become the defendant in a variety of human ailment lawsuits, along with the other major tobacco producers. American's strategic policy of diversification is clearly aimed at preserving its long-term prospects for profits in the presence of not only competition from the larger players in the tobacco industry, but also from legal and social pressures.

American Brands' annual reports provide strong evidence of the company's continuing strategy of diversification. By 1985, American's capital expenditures for its tobacco products had declined to 37 percent of the corporation's total capital expenditures. Capital expenditures say more about a company's long-range plans than any other set of statistics in its annual report, and are about as revealing a glimpse of the company's strategic plan that one can ordinarily get from an annual report. If the majority of American's present business is tobacco, its capital expenditures in the mid-1980s suggest that it is not likely to continue to be the majority indefinitely.

Has the strategy paid off? Well, it remains to be seen how the company's tobacco and nontobacco lines will fare over the long haul, but the diversification strategy surely hasn't hurt the company in the meantime. American was 78th in sales among the 1986 list of Fortune 500 largest industrial corporations, but was much higher in net income—40th. It was also toward the top of the Fortune list in several other important categories of profitability: net income as a percent of sales (9%), net income as a percent of stockholders' equity (17%), annual growth in earnings per share over the decade ending in 1985 (10%), and rate of total return to investors (18%) over that decade.

The way in which American Brands has financed its diversification program is especially noteworthy. A review of the company's annual reports from 1975 to 1985 reveals a significant reduction in the firm's leverage. In 1975, the firm had 82 cents of debt (short- and long-term) for every dollar of equity (common stock and convertible preferred). By 1985 the ratio had declined to 47 cents of debt for every dollar of equity. American's total debt actually increased slightly during this period, but the firm's equity more than doubled, primarily from the growth in its retained earnings that resulted from the firm's substantial profits—mostly profits from its tobacco lines. American has financed its diversion into nontobacco products mainly from the profits from its tobacco operations.

In continuing this diversification program in the 1980s, American has also reduced its cash holdings significantly. In 1985, the firm had a cash balance of $26.6 million, not even one-third the level just five years earlier. Its working capital was still more than $770 million and its current ratio over 1.5, levels that are generally regarded as in the safe range. Given American's healthy returns on its productive assets, the firm is clearly better off not having large amounts tied up in cash.

Many object strenuously to the idea of a firm's making large profits at the expense of people's health. The industry responds by claiming that the health questions are not yet settled; in the meantime, consumers are advised of the health risks on each pack of cigarettes.

American is, of course, not alone among producers of tobacco products in having to defend itself against adversaries in the courts and in other public arenas. Nor is it still alone in its strategy of diversifying away from its tobacco lines—R.J. Reynolds, for example, acquired Nabisco Brands in 1985 and renamed itself RJR Nabisco. American was clearly alone, however, when it pioneered the planning and execution of a profitable strategy of reduced reliance on a product that has become so shrouded in controversy.

BERKSHIRE HATHAWAY: THE POWER OF SEGMENT ANALYSIS

American's 1985 net income of $421 million was surpassed by a company with a far less profitable history—Berkshire Hathaway, Inc. That's no criticism of American Brands; among the Fortune 1000 industrial and service companies, none can match Berkshire Hathaway's record of sustained growth in profitability over the period 1975 to 1985. In 1975, the company earned $4.79 per share; 10 years later it earned $379.99 per share. An investor who purchased $10,000 worth of Berkshire Hathaway common stock in 1975 would have accumulated $592,600 in capital gains, dividends, and principal by 1985—more than a 50 percent annual return on investment!

To really understand Berkshire, one must know about its chairman, Warren Buffett. Buffett took the company over in 1965, at the age of 34. At that time, Berkshire Hathaway was a modest-size New England textile firm. By the end of 1985, it was a conglomerate earning $436 million and worth more than $2 billion, with substantial holdings of stock in the GEICO Corporation, The Washington Post, American Broadcasting Companies, and the Beatrice Companies. Sixteen years after buying the Berkshire Hathaway textile firm, Buffett had fully liquidated the company's textile holdings.

Buffett is living proof that a moderate Democrat working out of a humble office in Omaha, Nebraska, using tools not even as sophisticated as a calculator, can outperform an army of Wall Street investment analysts running elaborate mathematical models on mainframe computers.

He is also living proof of the power of straight-ahead segment analysis. Buffett and his vice chairman, Charles Munger, focus primarily on the numbers that break down Berkshire's profits by source. In the company's annual report for 1985 Buffett writes: "These numbers, along with far more detailed sub-segment numbers, are the ones that Charlie and I focus upon. We do not find consolidated figures an aid in either managing or evaluating Berkshire and, in fact, never prepare them for internal use."

Buffett describes his company as three businesses and a holding company. The three businesses—Nebraska Furniture Mart, See's Candy Shops, and the Buffalo Evening News—contribute less to Berkshire's bottom line than do the returns from the company's holdings of other corporations; but Buffett's skillful use of segment data to manage Berkshire's business side is no less evident than it is on the holding company side. From 1970 to 1985 the pretax earnings of Berkshire's three businesses grew, in the aggregate, from $8 million to $72 million. He offers a simple explanation for this management success:

> At Berkshire . . . we use an incentive–compensation system that rewards key managers for meeting targets in their own bailiwicks. If See's does well, that does not produce incentive compensation at the News—or vice versa. Neither do we look at the price of Berkshire stock when we write bonus checks. We believe good unit performance should be rewarded whether Berkshire stock rises, falls, or stays even. Similarly, we think average performance should earn no special rewards even if our stock should soar. "Performance," furthermore, is defined in different ways depending upon the underlying economics of the business: in some our managers enjoy tailwinds not of their own making, in others they fight unavoidable headwinds.

These incentives can be substantial. Berkshire's top managers occasionally receive incentive bonuses as large as five times their base salaries, bonuses that can exceed $2 million.

Buffett devotes a good deal of his attention as well to the segment numbers on the holding company side of Berkshire's operations. At the end of 1985, Berkshire's largest holdings were in GEICO, an insurance company that targets the government employee market; its ownership of GEICO was worth nearly $600 million at that time. Buffett attended closely to GEICO's segment data in his 1985 report to Berkshire's stockholders:

> GEICO, 38%–owned by Berkshire, reported an excellent year in 1985 in premium growth and investment results, but a poor year—by its lofty standards—in underwriting. Private passenger auto and homeowners insurance were the only important lines in the industry whose results deteriorated significantly during the year. GEICO did not escape the trend, although its record was far better than that of virtually all its major competitors.

Buffett does not rely on numbers alone. His instincts about the people who manage the companies that he considers as prospective investments are no less important. But he will neither buy into a company nor continue to support one that has not "demonstrated consistent earning power."

Few companies have demonstrated the consistent earning power, and the sustained ability to expand profits, that Warren Buffett's Berkshire Hathaway has. His attention to the numbers is not the beginning and end of the story of his success, but it is clearly a crucial part of the story.

DIGITAL EQUIPMENT CORPORATION: PROFITING FROM EFFECTIVE COMMITMENTS TO R&D

If there were a hall of fame for creators of rags-to-riches corporations, alongside the bust of Warren Buffett would be that of

Kenneth Olsen. (*Fortune* magazine has called Olsen "arguably the most successful entrepreneur in the history of American business.") In 1957 Olsen raised $70,000 for the start-up venture, the Digital Equipment Corporation (DEC); by 1987, DEC was widely regarded as the only serious competition to the computer giant, IBM.

Olsen made DEC that way out of a remarkable combination of skill, effort, and resourcefulness: a thorough understanding of the technology; close contact with and interest in the customer; and managerial prowess in both good times and bad.

In the world of computers, DEC is known particularly for staying at the leading edge of the technology of high-speed communications between computers, that is, computer hardware and software systems that are connectable, integrated, or networked. These systems have been tailored to the specific needs of a variety of settings, including the office, the large industrial plant, stock exchange, hospital, utility company, financial institution, and the research laboratory.

One aspect of DEC's strategy stands out as key to the company's success: Olsen's aggressive and continuing commitment to keeping the company in front in product development. This commitment is revealed in the company's substantial investment in a variety of research and development projects. Expenditures on research and development at DEC ran pretty consistently in the neighborhood of 20 to 25 percent of gross profit from 1975 to 1986. At IBM, a company with a reputation for being more marketing-oriented and less research-oriented, R&D expenses were in the neighborhood of 15 percent of gross profit during that period.

As the computer industry competed itself into the doldrums of reduced profitability in the mid-1980s (many companies flat-out folded), DEC's profits more than doubled from 1983 to 1986, and showed no signs of turning down. Most industry observers attribute this feat to Olsen's commitment to developing hardware and software products that provide the best readily available means of moving information from one computer to another, even between ordinarily incompatible computers. Digital developed a reputation for providing the technology to enable users of large and small computers of the same brand to move data between the machines, technology that even the maker of the machines frequently was unable to provide.

Olsen's commitment to research and development may be the key to DEC's profitability, but he's distinguished himself from the pack of ordinary entrepreneurs for having the extraordinary ability to manage his company from its infancy to the status of one of the 100 largest of the Fortune 500 industrial corporations. (The 1986 Fortune list ranked DEC 55th in sales, 43rd in assets, 38th in net income, and 26th in stockholders' equity.) Steven Jobs of Apple Computer, Mitchell Kapor of Lotus Development, and a host of other extremely successful high-tech entrepreneurs found less of a knack for corporate management.

Digital and Olsen were most severely tested in 1983, when the company's profit numbers declined to $284 million from $417 million the previous year. Olsen, whose company had become a business school case study model for decentralized management, saw DEC's decentralization as the problem rather than as a solution, and quickly transformed the firm into a monolith, to the extreme discomfort of many of the company's top managers. Critics who had written off Olsen as yet another technology genius who didn't know how to manage watched DEC's profits again soar and Olsen's position become ever more secure.

For Olsen, managing DEC toward still greater profitability means a continuing commitment to the future and continuing investment in R&D. Digital's quest to advance the frontier of ever faster, more efficient information processing technology in the workplace continues. In DEC's 1986 annual report Olsen writes:

Our goal is to connect all parts of an organization—the office, the factory floor, the laboratory, the engineering department—from the desktop to the data center. We can connect everything within a building; we can connect a group of buildings on the same site or at remote sites; we can connect an entire organization around the world. We propose to connect a company from top to bottom with a single network that includes the shipping clerk, the secretary, the manager, the vice president, even the president.

Ken Olsen, in short, doesn't think only about business in the current quarter. "A New Englander," he says, "doesn't worry about next winter; he worries about the winter after."

GIANT FOOD: PROFITING FROM INNOVATION, CONSUMERISM, AND A COMMITMENT TO DISCIPLINED PLANNING AND CONTROL

Kenneth Olsen isn't the only successful businessperson who thinks about the next two winters. Israel Cohen and David Sykes, respectively CEO and CFO of Giant Food, Inc., in fact think carefully about the next three. More about that in a moment; first a word about the grocery business.

Israel Cohen's father, Nehemiah, opened the first Giant store in the District of Columbia in 1936, with his partner, Samuel Lehrman. If the store had a distinctive characteristic, it was customer service—the elder Cohen said that the three keys to success were people, people, and people. The half century that followed saw the transformation of the grocery business from the simple mom-and-pop operation era, through the emergence of the dominant supermarket chain stores of the 1950s and 1960s, to the era of the highly computerized food chain of the 1980s—from no-tech to low-tech to high-tech. And from one store in the District to over 140 throughout D.C., suburban Virginia, Maryland, and Baltimore, financed primarily from the profits of the company's extraordinarily well-managed operations.

The 50 years of profitability and growth did not, however, change Giant's fundamental focus on serving the customer. Giant Food's staff (Cohen calls them his "associates") are extremely friendly, its aisles are kept immaculately clean, its lighting bright, its displays tasteful, its shelves well-stocked (with back-up inventories stored overhead to facilitate replacement and reduce back-room misplacement and damage), and its goods very competitively priced.

In the early 1980s, Cohen directed the company's interest in service toward the development of gourmet food stores for the Washington area's expansive affluent community, which resides in three of the highest income counties in the United States: Montgomery County, Maryland; and Fairfax and Arlington Counties, Virginia. After working out problems that inevitably occur with a prototype operation (one major problem was excessive labor costs, which the company effectively reduced from the unprofitable level of nearly 30 percent of sales to the profit-yielding level of about 20 percent), Giant built a number of gourmet markets that cater to that clientele's more cosmopolitan tastes: hundreds of varieties of wines and teas arranged by country, scores of international cheeses, pastas in every imaginable shape and color, and a delicatessen stocked with a bewildering variety of mouth-watering prepared dishes.

One of Giant's most revolutionary innovations was its companywide installation of computerized scanners in the late 1970s. Its two-to-three year lead over the competition in introducing this powerful rapid checkout technology into the chain supermarket business was instrumental in moving consumers from Safeway, A&P, and Giant's other competitors in the Washington area over to Giant Food. This increase in market share easily justified Giant's investment in the computerized scanners, but the scanners did much more: They accumulated data that permitted the company to monitor its inventory on a real-time basis and to replenish its inventory quickly with an automated ordering system, which has saved Giant millions each year in inventory carrying and management costs and in avoiding lost revenues associated with stock outages.

Another of Giant's highly profitable innovations is its successful use of vertical integration to reduce costs and improve internal control and efficiency. Giant Construction Company, the corporation's in-house construction division, carries out all new store construction and remodeling jobs, both on site and in its two-acre construction plant. Giant's in-house flower operation, which features a 30,000-square foot warehouse in suburban Maryland, is the largest flower operation on the East Coast; it efficiently supports Giant's more than 100 stores that have flower departments. The corporation also produces its own dairy and bakery products; operates its own soda bottling and ice cube plants; services its own equipment in the meat and other "front-end, point-of-sale" departments; maintains over 1000 vehicles; and runs its own warehouses.

If customer service is the binding constraint on Giant's profitability, and innovation and vertical integration its primary vehicles, Giant's commitment to effective planning and control, both short- and long-term, has been the heart and soul of its financial success. Cohen and Sykes manage the development of an annual profit plan—a detailed *pro forma* income statement that establishes targets right down to the level of each division and subdivision of the company—and a corresponding cash flow plan. Operations that don't perform up to profit standards are closed down. Some examples: Giant stores in Richmond, Virginia; a chain of blue jean stores; and some car wash and dry cleaning operations.

Cohen and Sykes also oversee the development of a capital

expenditure plan, Giant's detailed blueprint for growth over the longer term. And a detailed three-year plan for assets and the financing of asset growth and replacement.

Disciplined planning and control starts with the creation of each new store, which is accompanied by detailed projections of revenues and costs that are carefully reviewed by the corporate Management Committee. The projections are then used as a basis for control in subsequent visits to each site as it engages in operations.

The need for detailed information in an industry of wafer-thin profit margins is immense, and Giant has risen to the challenge. Sales data may be gathered as frequently as daily to test product promotions. Payroll data are forecast for each store department both in hours and dollars, and variances are scrutinized and acted upon weekly.

The payoff for such extraordinarily disciplined attention to pertinent details has been equally extraordinary. By the mid-1980s, Giant was easily the most profitable of the large, publicly held grocery chains. The company's net income of 20 percent of stockholders' equity and its 21 percent annual growth in earnings per share over the decade ending in 1985 were near the very top of the 1986 Fortune list of the 50 largest retailing companies. For the decade ending in 1985, Giant earned a whopping 40 percent average annual return for its investors, including both dividends and stock appreciation.

And its growth continues. Giant's net income more than tripled from 1981 to 1986, from $18 million to more than $57 million; its equity more than doubled during the same period, and its assets nearly doubled. The tenfold increase in its stock price during that 5-year period suggests that stockholders anticipated more of the same for some years to come.

What may be Giant Food's most significant contribution to the world of commerce is that it dispels one of the pervasive myths of business: that a firm must emphasize either customer service or profitability numbers—it can't manage by the numbers and be people-oriented, too. Cohen is a shining example of the CEO who has managed to have both.

MARRIOTT CORPORATION: MORE ON INNOVATION, CONSUMERISM, AND DISCIPLINED PLANNING AND CONTROL

If Giant Food's formula for profitability is mirrored in another industry, the reflection is the Marriott Corporation in the business of lodging, restaurants, and contract food services. Marriott's commitment to serving the customer is suggested by its referring to its primary business as "hospitality." The commitment is more deeply expressed in the friendly faces that seem to be so much more common among the staff of Marriott hotels than among the staff in most competing hotels—from the managers to the folks behind the registration counter to the housekeepers in the hallways—and by the extraordinary growth of Marriott's hotel business.

Commitment to customer service begins at the top, with Marriott's chairman, J. W. (Bill) Marriott, Jr. Like Giant Food's Izzy Cohen, Bill Marriott inherited the legacy of customer service from his father, J. Willard Marriott, Sr., who started the company in 1927 in the form of a small root beer stand just a few blocks from where Nehemiah Cohen would build his first grocery store a few years later. The root beer stand evolved into a major mid-Atlantic restaurant chain, Hot Shoppes. In the late 1930s, Marriott started preparing box lunches for the airlines, and soon became the largest independent airline caterer.

Bill Jr. joined the company in 1956. Soon afterwards he brought it into the hotel business by opening the Twin Bridges Motor Hotel in Rosslyn, Virginia. He became Marriott's president in 1964, and in time expanded the company's holdings substantially. By 1987, Marriott ran over 200 hotels, owned some 700 restaurants (adding the Big Boy and Roy Rogers chains to the Hot Shoppes), franchised about 1000 more restaurants in the United States and abroad, and dominated the airline and airport catering service and college cafeteria markets.

Marriott's consistent selection of winning new ventures is not solely the product of good luck. It derives largely from effective financial analysis, beginning with a sophisticated assessment of the profit projections of each prospect. Marriott's financial officers, among the most capable within the Fortune 1000 companies, subject each major capital investment prospect to intensive scrutiny—first, in terms of a carefully developed projection of the investment's profit stream and the ability of the net present value of that stream to surpass the corporate hurdle rate.

The prospects that survive the net present value test are then set up as prototypes and tested in the real world. The financial performance of the prototype is subjected to rigorous examination. If it passes that test, it becomes a bona fide corporate profit center.

The innovative successes that have survived this extensive screening process quickly became well known in the industry —Marriott's Courtyard hotels, all-suite hotels, and life-care communities for the elderly are some prominent examples. The corporation's extremely successful Courtyard hotels operation, for example, started with projections on paper; the concept moved to three prototype models in Atlanta in the fall of 1983; by 1987, 40 were in operation, with 300 planned for the early 1990s.

The real secret to Marriott's profitability, however, may have as much to do with the expeditious way that the company handles prospects that are *not* proudly described in the company's annual report, that is, the prospects that didn't survive the company's thorough screening process. Marriott's Great America theme parks of the late 1970s, for example, while they

passed the net present value test, never got beyond two prototypes (in the Chicago and San Francisco areas) with the company.

How did the reality about theme parks fall short of the projections? Primarily in two respects. First, the projections did
not have the benefit of hindsight knowledge about how capital
intensive a competitive theme park would turn out to be. To
attract crowds at a profitably high price year after year, the
company learned that a major, invariably expensive new attrac-
tion would have to be added frequently. Second, the projections did not anticipate the glut of competing parks that would
arise after Marriott had already committed to the two prototype
parks, competition that reduced revenues and squeezed the
projected profit margins down to levels that fell short of the
company's high standards. While others stayed in the theme
park business, Marriott profitably divested its theme parks by
1985.

Marriott's reluctance to tie up capital excessively has paid off
in other areas, too. Starting in the late 1970's, Marriott syndi-
cated much of its hotel holdings off of its balance sheet, selling
the assets to partnerships and maintaining control of the hotel
operations through 25- to 50-year management contracts. This
move helped Marriott's stockholders by allowing the company
to realize appreciation in its real estate holdings, while eliminating depreciation and interest costs, thus increasing reported
earings and making the stock more attractive.

Bill Marriott's principal management vehicle is the company's budgeting system. Marriott uses the budget as his com-
mand-and-control system by sitting down with each senior
executive line officer periodically to review both the variances
of the recent actuals from the budgeted numbers and the budget projections for the coming period. While these sessions
tend to be more congenial and supportive than they are con-
frontational, they are thorough.

This direct and conscientious involvement of the CEO in the process of planning and control allows the company to respond quickly and effectively to problems as they occur. More importantly, it deepens the commitment of the entire company to producing tangible results.

The payoff from this combination—emphasis on customer service, scrutiny of the numbers associated with new ventures, and commitment to the budgeting process—is as extraordinary as the process itself. Marriott kept its return on equity at or above 20 percent throughout the period 1980 to 1986. It increased its earnings per share 25 percent annually for the decade ending in 1985 (fifth among the Fortune 50 retailing companies). Its total return to investors for that period averaged 22 percent per year.

Marriott has succeeded by sticking to the business it knows best—hospitality. It has succeeded also by paying close attention to the numbers.

EATON CORPORATION: MANAGING WITH FINANCIAL FORECASTS

In 1911 Joseph Oriel Eaton entered what was then a high-tech industry: axles for the horseless carriage. Like today's advanced technology company, the Eaton Axle & Spring Company became aware before long of the need to diversify; so it added allied markets in the 1920s: truck axles, passenger car components, and parts for aircraft engines. After that came truck transmissions, automotive fluid power products, hydraulic motors and hydrostatic transmissions, and a variety of machine products from the simple to the highly engineered.

In the late 1970s, under chairman E.M. deWindt, Eaton carried forward its strategy of diversification by acquiring for the first time firms outside of the machinery business, in the electronics and electrical power management industries. Eaton is now a major player in aerospace and defense electronics.

The centerpiece of Eaton's diversification strategy is the strategic forecast. Its decision to move into electronics was based on the forecast of an especially high rate of growth in capital investments in electrical equipment. Those forecasts were not wrong. By the mid-1980s, the Eaton's electronics revenues were growing at the rate of about 20 percent per year, while profits from its electronics business were increasing by between 34 percent to 100 percent per year.

Rigorous forecasting is crucial at Eaton also as a tool for controlling operations. Each corporate division updates a 12-month rolling forecast at the middle of each month; by the end of the month, the forecast of the current month's activity is updated. These forecasts include details of both the income statement and balance sheet.

Eaton combines these financial forecasts with solid segment analysis. Its management responded to the 1982 recession by streamlining its weakest segments, including the unloading of its forestry equipment and hoist equipment lines and its lift truck operations. By the time of its 1985 annual report, it was able to give a much more positive assessment to its stockholders: "Given the good returns from our very efficient vehicle components businesses, full profit parity between segments is an ambitious goal, and one that will require time and steadfast management. Eaton is committed to provide both."

Eaton's reliance on financial forecasting and segment analysis for management decisions clearly contributes to its position as one of the 100 most profitable industrial corporations in the United States (its $231 million of profit was 71st on the Fortune 500 list for 1985). Over the decade ending in 1985, Eaton returned its stockholders over 16 percent annually in dividends and stock appreciation; it also grew its earnings per share at an impressive 15 percent annual rate during that period.

KELLOGG COMPANY: HOW TO PROFIT FROM THE RETIREMENT OF EQUITY

The Kellogg Company of Battle Creek, Michigan—maker of Kellogg's Corn Flakes, Rice Krispies, Frosted Flakes, and a host of other products whose names are known by children of all ages—has profitability numbers very similar to those of Eaton's: $281 million in profit in 1985 (61st on the Fortune 500 industrials list); 18 percent total return to stockholders over the period 1975–1985; and 13 percent annual increase in earnings per share during that period.

Kellogg's legacy began about the same time as Eaton's—1906, when Will Keith Kellogg combined his entrepreneurial flair with his brother's practical inventiveness to form the Kellogg Company. A significant early contribution of the Kellogg brothers' to diet trends, both here and abroad, was the creation, development, and effective marketing of the corn flake. Over the years, Kellogg's Corn Flakes remained the very model of the company's general strategy of running a profitable business based on the manufacture and sale of grain-based food products that were nutritious and tasty alternatives to the public's more traditional heavy and fat-laden meals.

Today, as in the early part of the 20th century, the company markets only food items, but the offering is much broader: ready-to-eat cereals, frozen pies and waffles, toaster pastries, soups and soup bases, tea, yogurt, and snack items. And it reaches a much larger community; its products are manufactured in 18 countries and distributed in 130 countries.

An important part of Kellogg's financial success, some 80 years after its creation, derived from its concentrating on what it had always done best: breakfast cereals. Its CEO, William LaMothe, is a crusader for whole-grain consumption as a pathway to the health of both the public and the Kellogg Company. The consumption of breakfast cereal rose to an all-time high of nine pounds per person per year by the mid-1980s, largely at the expense of the consumption of red meat, and LaMothe is determined to increase it further: "A lot of areas are close to 13 pounds. Why not make the whole country average 13?"*

An aspect of LaMothe's direction that may have contributed no less to Kellogg's profitability than his marketing leadership has been the company's effective financial management. While Kellogg's revenues, assets, and profits grew steadily during the decade ending in 1985, its annual reports reveal a sharp decline in stockholders' equity starting in 1984: from $978 million in 1983 to $683 million in 1985 (it had dropped to $487 million in 1984!). Between 1983 and 1985, the number of shares outstanding declined by 20 percent, from 153 million to 123 million. Meanwhile, long-term debt jumped more than 20-fold, from $19 million in 1983 to $393 million in 1985 (consisting mostly of $200 million in Eurodollar notes and $149 million in bonds). Traditionally a fairly conservative financial operation, Kellogg discovered leverage in the mid-1980s.

How did this shift from equity to debt help the bottom line? Largely by replacing dividends, which are not a tax-deductible expense, with interest, which is. From 1983 to 1985, Kellogg's dividend payments declined from $124 million to $111 million while its interest expense increased from $7 million to $35 million. At the company's 46 percent tax rate, a $23 million shift from dividends to interest adds $10.6 million to aftertax profit. And while decreasing total dividend payments by this $23 million amount, the company was nonetheless able to increase its dividends per share by a modest two percent during the 2-year period!

Kellogg's shareholders were undoubtedly pleased to have more aftertax earnings available for dividends and corporate growth, but the retirement of corporate equity enhanced their investment in an even more immediate way as well. The com-

---

* Quote is from Jack Willoughby's article in *Forbes*, "The Snap, Crackle, Pop Defense" (March 25, 1985), p. 86.

pany's purchase of 20 percent of the outstanding shares in the open market represented an increase in the demand for the stock, an increase that clearly contributed to the doubling of the price of the stock from year-end 1983 to year-end 1985 (from $17 to $35).

Trading corporate equity for debt was a major phenomenon during the 1980s, not restricted to the Kellogg Company. Most corporations did so at least partly to make themselves less appealing to prospective corporate raiders: by raising the price of common voting shares, by increasing debt-to-equity ratios, and by ridding the balance sheet of relatively unproductive yet attractive liquid assets. Kellogg's was not immune from those pressures. Its level of working capital, in the neighborhood of $300 million throughout the period from 1979 to 1983, dropped to $87 million in 1984 and stayed well under $200 million by year-end 1985.

While protecting themselves in the near term, LaMothe and his associates clearly kept their eyes on Kellogg's future during the turbulent period of corporate takeovers in the mid-1980s. Kellogg's capital expenditures grew from $157 million for 1983 to $246 million for 1985, with investments worldwide in new technology and facilities. Major capital projects included the construction of prototype year 2000 cereal manufacturing facilities in Canada and Wales, and a major modernization of Kellogg's flagship cereal production facility in Battle Creek.

The Kellogg Company was one of the strongest corporations in the country in 1987, with little to indicate that it would not keep getting stronger for some time.

USG: USING NUMBERS TO SUSTAIN PROFITABILITY IN A VOLATILE INDUSTRY

The Kellogg Company isn't the only one that has profited by building a major conglomerate within a single industry (food) deliberately on a successful basic product line (breakfast cereal). The USG Corporation has profited by constructing a major building products conglomerate deliberately on an equally successful basic product line—gypsum board. Gypsum board is the plaster mineral used in more than 90 percent of all interior walls and ceilings in modern homes, and the vast majority in today's commercial buildings and in wall and ceiling replacements. USG has long been the dominant producer of gypsum board, and its dominance has been effectively extended to other quarters of the building products industry.

The USG Corporation, established officially in January 1985, is a holding company that evolved from the United States Gypsum Company. The newer entity operates eight subsidiaries including: United States Gypsum Company, the world's largest producer of gypsum products; Masonite Corporation, the largest producer of wood fiber products for interior paneling, exterior siding, and roofing; USG Acoustical Products Company, a leading maker of mineral fiber ceiling and insulation products; and five other construction-related companies. In the mid-1980s, about half of USG's total revenues came from the sale of gypsum products.

USG has been extremely successful with those product lines. Here are some of the impressive numbers: $224 million in net income in 1985 (73rd among the Fortune 500 industrials); net income as a percent of stockholders' equity of 23 percent (41st); 23 percent annual growth in earnings per share over the decade ending in 1985 (27th); and a 26 percent rate of total return to investors for the decade (64th).

A key to USG's profitability has been its ability to expand its gross profit margin. In 1975, gross profits were 18.7 percent of sales; by 1980, they were at 21.1 percent; by 1985, 28.4 percent. For every dollar of sales, USG thus had available 52 percent more for both its operating costs and for the bottom line in 1985 than in 1975.

How did the company pull off these extraordinary feats?

Primarily in two ways. It did so, first, by tracking tried-and-true numbers of business performance by subsidiary, especially gross and net profit margins, and growth rates in sales, and by holding its managers accountable for achieving or surpassing target levels. By tying managers' incentive bonuses closely to the numbers, USG provided, and continues to provide, strong inducements to improve the corporation's bottom line in the aggregate.

Its profitability resulted, second, from its continually adding strong companies that fit well with USG's existing lines and its divesting the weaker units. (In 1985, for example, it beefed up its acoustical product line by acquiring the assets of Conwed Corporation, and it divested itself of the Hollytex Carpet Mills, Inc, Peeters Carpets Ltd., and the Gossen Division of USG Industries, Inc.). The effectiveness of USG's highly selective strategy of acquisition and divestiture was accomplished largely by subjecting those decisions to an uncommonly rigorous analysis. USG relies on detailed projections of profit and cash flow streams for each prospective acquisition; it then calculates net present values and internal rates of return to provide an informed basis for choosing among the prospects.

Robert Day and Eugene Miller, elected CEO and CFO of the corporation in 1985, are determined to move USG to still higher levels of performance. Over the years, the building products industry has had one chronic problem: extreme cyclical demand. The industry has been buffeted to a much greater degree than most industries by the shifting winds of economic conditions, due primarily to fluctuations in interest rates and business conditions and shifts in tax policy and in the demographics of the family.

Day and Miller have responded by making strategic planning a major management priority for the coming years. They created a vice president-level director of strategic planning and corporate development and a highly motivated planning department, and they immersed over 100 of the company's managers in intensive seminars on strategic planning. Day's report to the stockholders includes a thoughtful assessment of the factors that influence the construction business cycle. It also describes the strength of the repair and remodel market (over $150 billion, with 10 to 12 percent average annual growth) and USG's strategy of filling the troughs in the construction business cycle by pushing the company's repair and remodeling lines.

In 1986, USG's primary strategic goals were to: (1) maintain or increase its market position in its mainstream gypsum and hardboard businesses; (2) increase the aftertax return on capital in all units; (3) increase corporate emphasis on research to develop major new products; and (4) improve earnings and growth through acquisitions that leverage current corporate strengths.

It remains to be seen whether USG will achieve these goals and continue on its fast profit track. The company's proven ability to focus on the right numbers and plan effectively should discourage bets against the company's future.

12

IMPROVING THE BOTTOM LINE: THE SMALL COMPANY

. . . a majority of small firms do not normally have the opportunity to publicly sell issues of stocks or bonds in order to raise funds. . . . On the other hand, many financial problems facing the small firm are very similar to those of larger corporations.

—U.S. SMALL BUSINESS ADMINISTRATION

Fortune 1000 corporations don't have a patent on the technology of profiting from the effective use of financial data. Small- and medium-size companies are, more than ever, becoming sophisticated about bottom-line financial management, too. In this chapter we'll look at a few.

First, a few words about small businesses. (They're often referred to euphemistically as growing businesses, but hundreds of thousands of small businesses expire each year; moreover, some of the most spectacular business growth in the world takes place in large corporations.) The Small Business Administration reports the existence of more than 13 million businesses of all sizes in the United States in 1986. Most of those are small, hoping-to-prosper companies with no more than a handful of employees, modest profits, and a single location, often the home.

The small business can be characterized in only one way: It defies any single characterization. Some small businesses perform services; some sell goods; and some do both. Those that sell goods include manufacturers, brokers, and retailers. Many firms are proprietorships; many are partnerships; and many, corporations. Most are unique operations serving a particular niche market, but many are franchises, operating out of a formula that has proven successful elsewhere.

One important resource is required of all businesses, large and small: financial data. It's needed for tax reporting; it's needed to obtain funding from banks and investors; and it's needed to provide information to stockholders about how their investment in the company is doing. Many owners of small businesses are aware of the potential for using financial data also to improve profitability, as we've seen the big guys do in the preceding chapter. Some of them fail, anyway—for focusing on the wrong numbers, or for not taking action that may be suggested by the numbers. Firms that do use them, however, are at a decided advantage, since the financial data are a proven useful management resource.

Okay, let's examine a few now. All are fictionalized accounts of real firms, fictionalized to protect the typically confidential nature of the closely held company.

THE INTERIOR DESIGN FIRM

Karen Barnes and Laura French, two respected and successful designers, decided, in the depths of the recession in late 1981, to combine their strengths and form an interior design firm in an affluent suburb of a large city. Initially, they sold window treatments (verticals and miniblinds, shades, and insulated window coverings) out of their homes while preparing to move into an office. The move after six months raised their costs significantly, making it difficult to compete with others selling window treatments out of their homes; but that loss was small when compared to the substantial gain to their credibility and the establishment of a base of operations out of which they could launch what would eventually turn out to be a major commercial and residential design business.

The early years weren't easy. Karen and Laura worked without pay for over a year to build the business. The local newspapers gave them good public relations ink in some feature articles, but marketing the new enterprise turned out to be expensive and frustratingly slow to produce the desired results. Some commercial markets that looked attractive on the surface, like the entrance lobbies and common areas of the city's toney condominiums, turned up a few profitable clients, but resulted mostly in jobs that too often got bogged down in indecisive condominium committees.

Other problems were even more vexing. Laura's ownership of the space that was rented to the business, together with the question of setting a rental rate that would satisfy both her financial needs and those of the business, combined to pose an awkward problem. Expansion into an adjacent space bought by the partners at the end of the second year strained the firm's cash flow. And a third partner, Marilyn, primarily responsible for the firm's early marketing efforts, left the business in year three because the growing pressures of the firm intruded too much into her family responsibilities. Finding a fair market value to buy out Marilyn's shares in the corporation, as well as her interests in the new property, ended up consuming much more time, emotional energy, and legal costs than either Karen or Laura had envisioned.

Karen and Laura were too determined to succeed, however, to allow themselves to be overcome by the false starts and frustrations that all new and eventually successful businesses encounter. Out of their determination for financial success, it quickly became clear that they needed a detailed and accurate accounting of how each aspect of their business was doing.

They began by adding to their already useful client and vendor files a general ledger that provided details of revenues and the cost of sales for each product and service line, and a fairly detailed accounting of operating expenses. They first divided their operations into their three primary markets: commercial design, residential design, and a walk-in showroom and store. They further divided those primary markets into basic components: design fees, furniture, fabrics (for upholstery, drapery, and bedspreads), wallpaper, carpeting, and artwork. This organization of their financial data empowered the partners to systematically track the performance of each segment of their business.

Then they were fortunate enough to find Sonya, an extremely competent and dedicated controller, to manage the firm's finances. Sonya acquired a computer and a straightforward accounting software package for the firm, and began providing information that permitted Karen and Laura to improve the firm's ability to achieve its bottom-line goal: increasing the salaries of the principals and staff while maintaining the firm's profits at a modest level.

Sonya's numbers were eye-opening. The firm's showroom-store segment, intended as a profit center that would also serve as a marketing tool by bringing walk-in clients and prospects to the business, revealed itself instead to be a loss center that brought in many more limited prospects and small customers than it did the kinds of upscale clients the firm targeted. By expeditiously closing the store in 1984, Karen and Laura not only gained needed design space, but were freed up to concentrate more on the firm's primary business, high-class design. This enabled them to significantly increase the firm's gross profits (from $85,000 in 1983 to $210,000 in 1985).

By the end of 1986, the firm had reached $1 million in revenues and $300,000 of gross profits, the vast majority of which went to cover the salaries of the two principals, their comptroller, a receptionist, and two part-time designers. In 1987, to further secure their claim as one of the truly prestige design firms in the area, the firm upgraded its staff of designers and became more selective about the projects it took on.

Karen and Laura's interior design corporation is not destined to become a Fortune 500 service company. It already has proven to be a financially healthy firm, however. And with the principals' positive view of themselves and their mission, and their attention to the numbers, the firm shows every sign of doing even better for some time to come.

THE HEALTH CARE SOFTWARE FIRM

An industry that offers considerably brighter prospects for growth of the firm, and opportunities for failure on a grander scale as well, is the computer software industry. The rapid and phenomenal growth in the mid-1980s of such companies as Lotus Development, Ashton-Tate, Microsoft, and Borland International serves as vivid proof of the upside potential of this business. Companies with good software products and effective marketing strategies have quickly turned a battalion of young and adventurous techies into millionaires.

Many software entrepreneurs were able to achieve corporate stardom by targeting their products to a niche. One prominent example is Sandra Kurtzig, CEO of Ask Corporation, who made millions from the development of a computerized materials requirements planning (MRP) system that schedules resources for manufacturing companies. Another is Andrew Tobias, who made a small fortune from his personal finance software. Others made fortunes by targeting on computer-aided design software, legal research and document retrieval software, and securities trading software.

Jeffrey Thompson set out to capture another important niche

market: software focused on tracking patients through the health care system. (Sandra Kurtzig and Andrew Tobias are real people; Jeffrey Thompson isn't.) Thompson started by organizing a corporation in 1972 and winning a large federal grant to develop a patient-tracking system for large county health care facilities. This complex public domain software system proved to be a boon to large hospitals throughout the country, hospitals that had become increasingly frustrated about misplacing bulky patient files and thus subjecting themselves to diagnosis and treatment errors and major medical malpractice suites. Thompson's system automated the essential data about each patient's case and scheduled event, noting outcomes and their dates as they occurred. It also produced reports about aggregate case loads and hospital system performance for hospital managers. The system was promoted by the federal government through block grants to the states. It soon became the country's dominant patient-tracking software system.

Aware that the expertise that developed the system could be put to much more profitable uses, Thompson used his firm's resources to create a proprietary and advanced version of the public domain software in 1982—fortuitously, at about the same time that the federal government eliminated its block grants for state health care programs—and he set out to market this more advanced product directly to the local hospitals at a commercial price.

His company was, however, very thinly capitalized; it would have been unable to carry its staff of over 100 programmers, managers, and support people were it not for another apparently fortuitous event—a $10 million contract the company received at the end of 1982 to install the software in a major federal hospital system.

The federal contract bought time for Thompson to create a marketing capability to sell the software directly to hospitals; it also bought time for him to get additional capital to further improve the software and create new markets with modified versions of the software. Thompson soon discovered that venture capitalists were intrigued by the prospects of his company, but they needed some assurance that improvements could be made in three areas: (1) assembly of a professional marketing team to substantially increase the firm's nonfederal revenues; (2) creation of an effective corporate control structure to streamline the organization and improve its ability to execute a plan; and (3) development of a viable financial capability.

Thompson was able to put together a business plan with extremely detailed financial projections that attracted $1 million in venture capital in 1983. Bringing in this needed equity reduced his share of corporate ownership to 65 percent, still more than enough to maintain control of the company.

The following year was disastrous. The software sales predicted in Thompson's business plan did not materialize; the hospitals were accustomed to receiving the software and support for free and balked at the commercial price, even though it was in line with the prices of systems of similar complexity sold elsewhere. The company's diversification plan was only marginally successful. Relations with the government project monitor on the $10 million federal contract went from not very good to terrible, despite the company's admirable performance on a difficult contract. Venture capitalists were not interested in helping Thompson without taking over the company; they experienced huge losses in 1984 throughout the high technology industries, and turned away from that market just as quickly as they had been attracted to it a couple of years earlier.

Thompson's fuel tank of liquid reserves was beginning to run on fumes. He had grown too attached to directing the organization he gave birth to nearly 15 years earlier to save it in the short term by accepting buy-out offers from larger software houses and venture capitalists. The company found itself grasping at straws: trying desperately to close sales that didn't materialize; putting off its creditors; working aggressively to collect its receivables; selling off assets; terminating equipment leases; and barely meeting each payroll, occasionally by postponing the offiers' paychecks until the cash was there.

A bank holding a large secured note grew increasingly worried and eventually called the note, sending the company into the bankruptcy court; Thompson quickly filed for protection from the company's creditors under the Chapter 11 provision of the Federal Bankruptcy Act.

What's the lesson here? A basic one is that detailed financial projections should not be mistaken for accurate ones. Thompson's projections were way off in two respects: (1) they did not account for the degree to which a small company with a single large client would be vulnerable to that client's misbehavior; and (2) they substantially overestimated the demand in their primary market, even before the problems caused by their federal government project monitor. There was no way the company could sustain such a double whammy.

Chapter 11 contains provisions for the court to hold off the creditors while the company prepares and executes a plan for corporate reorganization, and Thompson is using this protection to try to fix the problem. He has begun by seeking recovery of funds owed the company by the federal government under the problematic $10 million contract. He's also trying to develop a more realistic business plan.

Although not trained in financial management, he has developed a deep understanding of the power that it provides as a tool for managing his company. With some luck, he could get the brass ring the second time around.

THE HEALTH FOOD MANUFACTURER

In 1982, Mabel Gaines observed that she was making more money putting in 15 hours a week as a private consultant on diet and nutrition than as a 40-hour per week salaried hospital dietician. She had hit upon a dietary formula of grains (wheat, rice, and oats), dry milk, and defatted nuts that did wonders, as either a food supplement or substitute, for both patients and people on diets. Mabel knew how to buy the raw food material —how to take advantage of discounts, how to identify fresh, high-quality ingredients—and whom to buy it from. So she quit her job and decided to put all of her energy into the more profitable use of her time.

Her new corporation started primitively. She purchased raw food materials from the grocery store rather than from a wholesaler. She recorded each financial transaction serially on yellow pads, without distinguishing general ledger accounts from receivables and payables. Her marketing operations were totally by the seat of the pants, with no plan, no targets, and thus no basis for assessing performance.

But she managed to operate a profitable business, anyway. Working out of her home for nearly a year, her company recorded $6000 in revenues per month, and only $1000 of costs, including both the cost of goods sold and operating expenses. Mabel cleared $60,000 in pretax profit her first year, drawing no salary.

Toward the end of fiscal year 1983, the company's first year, Mabel took a number of prudent steps: She moved into a small office, hired an assistant to answer the phone and help mix and package the product, and hired an accountant to set up a more conventionally organized general ledger and set of customer and vendor accounts. By the end of 1984, the company's revenues grew to $85,000, but the higher costs left Mabel with only $45,000 in pretax profit and salary—still not bad.

Mabel decided to go for the home run in 1985. She hired a pricey marketing consultant to advise her on how to make the company's sales really soar. His services reduced the company's retained earnings by $10,000. Mabel followed his advice and spent another $180,000 on a major television commercial and newspaper ad campaign, including payments for the services of creative writers and marketing representatives, and in travel costs. After all that, her company's 1985 revenues ended up a disappointing $110,000, less than half of its $235,000 in total costs. In the process, Mabel learned something about the need for more systematic planning and control of major expenditures.

Thus 1986 became the year of the hangover, the year to pay off the firm's sizable debt incurred the previous year. It was a year marked also by Mabel's appearance on national network television, exposure that contributed significantly to her company's $150,000 in revenue for the year.

Back on track, and wiser in the ways of financial management, Mabel developed a business plan built more solidly on her company's existing customer base. Her current business plan includes sending attractive mail-order flyers periodically to her loyal customers and to middle- and upper-income new mothers (she gets the lists from suburban hospitals); telephoning doctors and hospital dieticians regularly; and seeing to it that the media are aware of the effective use of her company's product in medical research projects. Her longer-term business plan includes a joint enterprise with a major banking company to develop and market a food bar counterpart of the company's basic product to augment the granulated version, and the development of two major markets that she knows well: nursing homes and hospitals. Mabel, the professional dietician, is becoming Mabel, the professional businesswoman.

THE RESTAURANT

Mark and Sheri Horvath had reached their mid-40s and found themselves asking the question so common to humans of that age: "Is this all there is?" Parents of a pair of teenage daughters, Mark was a 25-year bureaucrat with the state's department of agriculture, and Sheri had rejoined the labor force as a waitress at a popular restaurant five years ago, became head waitress within a year, and was now one of the best in the business. With their girls in the high school honor society and starting to think about college, the need for more income became increasingly evident to Mark and Sheri. The $100,000 they had accumulated in mutual funds over the years, together with Mark's eligibility for a substantial state pension, gave them enough of a wealth and income parachute to induce them to jump out of the airplane and start the business they had been thinking about for years—a restaurant.

They prepared for the enterprise by reading articles about the restaurant business and by talking at length to a good friend who owned two restaurants. They knew the risks: Most new restaurants fail within five years, making loans all but impossible for neophytes to get. And they knew about the hard work needed to run a profitable operation. Sheri had had 10 years of experience with two different workaholic restaurant managers. Mark had learned some basic principles of business from the MBA he earned in night school, and he loved to cook; but they both understood that knowing some business principles and knowing how to cook had only a little to do with making a good living from a restaurant.

They were also clear about the upside potential of the venture. There were no decent barbecue restaurants in the city, and they had developed a reputation for making absolutely sensational barbecued spareribs and chicken for dozens of people every year at the neighborhood Memorial Day picnic. They were intelligent people who had proven to themselves that they could succeed at just about anything they set their minds to. And they were ready for some excitement, ready to be their own bosses, yet properly apprehensive about the risks that the venture presented to their financial and emotional health.

So they set as their goal to create, within three years, a barbecue restaurant that would become both a civic institution and a profitable enterprise.

During the last three months at their old jobs they worked nights and weekends putting together a business plan, starting from their broad goal and working backward to the intricacies of start-up activities and costs, purchasing of food and supplies, menu-planning, inventory control and record-keeping, hiring help, and paying for rent and utilities. They found a good downtown location; submitted all the required applications with the city and county; paid a lawyer to set them up as a Chapter S corporation, so that they would have both the protections against personal liabilities that the corporation provides and the ability to report start-up losses on their personal tax returns; and put employment ads in two local papers for waiters, bussers, and kitchen help.

They capitalized the venture with $50,000 of their mutual fund holdings and another $25,000 from Mark's parents, and took their business plan and the accompanying 3-year *pro forma* income statements, balance sheets, and cash flow projections to several banks for an additional $75,000 loan. Predictably, the best the banks would offer was a $50,000 line of credit secured by their home. Needing $100,000 to start the business properly, they gritted their teeth and signed the papers with the bank.

After a month of renovating the space; purchasing a broiler and oven, pots and pans, blenders and mixers, and other kitchen equipment; developing the basic menu and experimenting with items on it; hiring an assistant manager (who was also assistant cook and dishwasher), four waiters (two men and two women), and two bussers, and purchasing food, the restaurant opened on February 2, with balloons and door prizes. And with the usual mistakes: The menu wasn't back from the printer on schedule, they ordered too many beef ribs and not enough pork ribs, and they weren't set up yet to handle credit card customers.

Within a few weeks, Mark and Sheri settled into a routine and learned how to adapt to situations as they came up. They don't open the restaurant for business until 11:00 A.M.—few people want barbecue for breakfast—but they're usually there by 8:00 A.M. to set up: making sure there's enough of each item of food, checking the barbecue sauce, placing orders with food suppliers, reviewing the calendar of "to-do's" for the day and for the rest of the week, updating the books, finding a replacement for the waitress who called in sick this morning, and so on.

After committing some costly errors, Mark learned to avoid deliveries during rush hours, so that he could carefully check each shipment to make sure he was getting all the food he was paying for and that it was fresh, and so that he could date-sort the inventories in dry storage, the refrigerator, and freezer, to minimize the total costs of outage and spoilage. And they learned tricks of the trade, like putting a 20 percent-off special up on the blackboard on potato salad when the supply of cole slaw was running low because customers were ordering an unusual amount.

Mark and Sheri learned also the central importance of their menu to their entire operation. They changed it several times during the first year, sometimes to refine the selection of items, sometimes to change the prices (for example, to better reflect the higher labor cost associated with foods that take longer to prepare), and sometimes to improve the descriptions of the offerings to make them much more attractive.

And they learned the importance of managing the cost of goods sold in a competitive business. After paying too much for potatoes from a particular supplier, Mark learned to frequently compare the prices his various suppliers charged him with the prices of the same items from other vendors. The couple made it a habit to dine out a couple of times a month at other restaurants, looking for new ideas about menu selection and format, food preparation and presentation, service, background music, smoking/no-smoking seating arrangements, and restaurant decor.

Most of that sort of adaptation was expected when Mark

and Sheri created their detailed business plan. Certain events weren't expected. Like when they got snowed in at Sheri's parents' home in Springfield for three days right after Thanksgiving following a freak blizzard, and couldn't open because George, the assistant manager, came down with the mumps at the same time. And when Barbara, a pretty good waitress, showed up uncharacteristically angry one especially busy day and caused two tables of customers to get up and walk out in the middle of their meals.

Mark and Sheri learned by experience that some problems just come up and cause unexpected losses, like freak blizzards and mumps, and others can be prevented, like waitresses who are only pretty good. After the Barbara incident, Sheri said to Mark, "Look, if we're going to be the best, we can't settle for help that isn't committed to a successful operation 100 percent of the time. If we have to pay 15 or 20 percent above the going rates for such people, then let's do it. I can't live with worrying about whether we can depend on waiters who aren't professionals." Thus they learned to be more selective.

Lessons learned notwithstanding, the approach of the restaurant's first anniversary did not bring with it the profits that Mark and Sheri had projected. Their costs were only a little higher than the targets, but their revenues were about 25 percent below the projections. The restaurant was not generating the profits that they sensed were possible, and Mark could not find the answer by poring over the numbers every day.

So they sat down with their friend, the owner of two successful restaurants, for several hours of scrutiny; he made some useful observations and gave them some important advice. He pointed to several areas of excess capacity in their operation. They were aware of a little excess capacity during the lunch and dinner peaks and a lot between 2:00 P.M. and 6:00 P.M. each day, but they had not considered the excess capacity of about 25 percent associated with their relatively slow rate of customer turnover during the peak meal hours. By adding two waiters they were able to increase both the quality of service and their turnover rate. By advertising reduced prices on food and beer from 3:00 P.M. to 6:00 P.M. on weekdays, they found that their attendance and profit margins improved fairly quickly. They discovered that the numbers can reveal problems, but that they needed to bring a little creative thinking to the game, too.

The real boost to their revenues and profits came with an extraordinary promotional angle and some good luck. Mark and Sheri were devoted fans of the local professional football team, some of whom frequented the restaurant. When the team made the playoffs, Mark traveled 400 miles with a mobile barbecue pit to prepare ribs for the entire team. They upset the home team, and the newspaper reported the next day that several players attributed the win largely to Mark's ribs. His loyalty to the team and his winning ribs thus became something of a civic institution.

Soon their problem was not excess capacity, but 15-minute waits for seating at lunchtime and 30- to 45-minute waits at dinner. By the end of year two, Mark and Sheri were earning decent salaries and an $80,000 profit, almost enough to cover the previous year's loss.

By the end of year three, their first $100,000 profit year, they were able to use their retained earnings, with a $100,000 match from the bank, to more than double their capacity by moving into the next-door space. Although not exactly the way they had projected it, Mark and Sheri appear to be achieving their goal.

THE COMMUNITY NEWSPAPER

Tony Grant and Pete Cahill were successful community news reporters with one of the largest newspapers in the country, but unhappy with what they viewed as the consistent lack of imagination of the editors to whom they reported. Their frustration climaxed in 1981; they decided to do it right themselves by starting their own community newspaper. Their specific idea was an unusually high-quality community service newspaper. They worked out some rough estimates and, feeling somewhat invincible, persuaded themselves that they could profitably run a biweekly newspaper that would be delivered free to some 25,000 households and commercial establishments in the community, with the revenues from ads more than enough to cover the projected costs.

They were also able to convince others. They didn't have enough personal capital to launch the venture, so they went to friends in the community, who were also frustrated by the poor quality of the existing newspaper coverage of events in the community and wealthy enough to support the cause. Over a 60-day period, Tony and Pete raised $100,000 from 20 supporters, including the $7500 that they each put up. They quit their posts with the large newspaper, hired a classy staff (which, including themselves, gave them an editor, publisher, managing editor, and general manager), had a terrific champagne and hors d'oeuvres launching party, and in October 1981 published the first edition. Two months later, still caught up in the hubris of their exciting new venture, they decided to go weekly, thus doubling their production costs just at the season in the newspaper business when advertising revenues are at their notorious low.

Four engineers in the locomotive, a crew of attendants in the nearly empty passenger cars, coal stoking the engine at full steam, and with no speed or fuel gauges, Tony and Pete went to the bank for a 90-day note that would straighten out the curve in the track ahead. Somehow, they got the note, but with revenues still running well below projections, they drew their cash account down to the last few pennies as early as March 1982.

The next several months were extremely bleak. Tony and

Pete passed up several paychecks and dug further into their shallow pockets to carry them through. They laid off two senior staff members. Pete, still committed to the success of the venture, joined the staff of a national newspaper headquartered downtown to put food on his family's table and pay for his children's college tuition bills. They consolidated the four prior executive positions into one.

Their board of directors decided to meet with Tony every month to review their progress. Although it seemed unreasonable at the time, the board members asked the principals just the kind of tough questons to which the two reporters-turned-entrepreneurs needed to come up with answers: "What were your revenues last month? Your costs? Why were the former so low and the latter still so high? What are you doing about it?" And the toughest question: "Does it really make sense to try to keep this thing going?"

Tony came to regard these sessions as maulings. At the same time, the naivete of his thinking the previous summer and fall, that the bottom line would somehow just automatically show profits, started to sink in. He discovered that he and Pete really didn't know the numbers—they only knew they had a problem when they ran out of cash—and it was killing the business. For fiscal year 1982, they lost $235,000 on $275,000 of revenues.

In August 1982 two important steps were taken to keep the operation alive. One was to hire Grace, a person with a track record in marketing and a solid business sense, as advertising director. The other was to start using the services of Ron, the accountant in the building, to help organize their books so they could track their performance and be able to come up with better answers to the board's questions. Grace steered the newspaper's revenues to $425,000 by the end of the second year. They lost another $145,000, but the accountant's numbers were indicating that the monthly losses were approaching zero.

The board was still not thrilled with the way things were

going. They put up with Tony's metaphor about battleships being slow to turn around only because they really did view the newspaper as one that provided a crucial service to the community, a service that would be dearly missed if the operation folded. They decided to offer Tony and Grace incentive bonuses based on the profits of the business.

It took two and a half years from launching for the operation to produce its first monthly profit; this time they had a more sedate party. They still ended their third year with a loss of $20,000, but the battleship really did appear to be turned around.

In the fourth year, they earned over $20,000 of pretax profit on over $1 million of revenues, despite some unexpected legal costs. Finally able to think again about growth, they started a second newspaper in a neighboring community.

The business prospered from the growth. In fiscal year 1986, they turned a profit of $100,000, largely from a doubling of revenues from the previous year, to over $2 million.

Tony still knows how to think like a reporter, but he also thinks like a businessman. He attends closely to the monthly income statements, watching revenue growth and the major cost components—printing, reporter, and art costs, for example—as a percentage of revenues. When confronted with such decisions as whether to have a 96- or 100-page newspaper on a given week, he thinks of the trade-off between the approximately $20,000 of added annual cost of each additional sheet of four pages, which comes right out of the bottom line, and the value that the four pages add to the quality of the product.

He understands that the quality of the newspaper contributes to its readership and, in turn, to the rates they can charge for advertising, but he also knows that quality beyond a certain level doesn't contribute much. He believes that the 35 percent of his compensation that resulted from the newspaper's profits last year provides a healthy degree of tension between his two-different-world interests as coexecutive manager and as editor of the paper.

For fiscal year 1987, the paper was headed for over $3 million in revenues and about $250,000 in profits; the business was about to start a third paper in another community; it was appraised at over $2.5 million; and Tony was finally beginning to experience the best of both worlds.

THE DENTISTRY PRACTICE

Twenty years ago, Adam Starr was a good student, raised to believe that he could either aim his education toward a profession or finish college and enter business. Becoming a professional was considered to be a more socially acceptable way of earning a living, so Adam chose a career in dentistry. Four years of college were followed by four years of dental school, and then three years of dental training in the Army. In 1973, Adam took a $35,000 note from the bank, hired an assistant, and opened a practice a few miles from the center of a large city.

Adam was a perfectionist, aspiring to nothing less than the very finest dental care that each patient could receive. He took care of every patient just as he would want to be treated himself. During his first five years, he scheduled up to seven patients per day and, with cancellations, would typically see no more than six, but on some days he would spend as many as four hours with a single patient.

His work was really impeccable. Fillings and crowns rarely broke or fell out, and were meticulously set so that food would not catch on them or get lodged in pockets. People who had experienced run-of-the-mill dentistry before coming to Adam immediately saw the difference.

Adam's brand of perfection did come at a price, however. Adam frequently went over the time allotted for a particular patient to deal with the inevitable unexpected problem, and the patients in the waiting room tended to be less understanding of those other patients' needs than their own. People appreciated the high quality of care that Adam delivered, and often referred their friends to him, but the somewhat inconvenient location of Adam's office and the large blocks of time out of the day that a trip to his office entailed kept his practice from booming.

Another set of factors, external to Adam's operation, was at least as harmful. The entire dental industry was suffering from a recession. Fluoridation had cut down considerably on cavities and the corresponding need for fillings and crowns. Federal subsidies for medical and dental training during the 1960s approximately doubled the number of professionals in both fields; meanwhile, more extensive use of paraprofessionals further reduced the demand for dentists' services. Dental technology, including high-speed drills and suction devices, made dental practice more capital intensive and expensive. And insurance price schedules put a lid on what dentists could charge for specific services; Adam was actually losing money on some services, spending more time and material to perform them at his level of excellence than the guidelines would pay for.

After 15 years of practice, Adam had grown proud of his insistence on delivering the highest quality of dentistry, and gratified by the results that that standard produced for his patients. At the same time, he had grown increasingly concerned about the fact that his income had not grown to the level of income of many of his peers. He attributed the fact that many of them drove new BMWs and Mercedes, while he drove a 3-year-old subcompact automobile, to their having compromised the standards of the profession.

Another voice in his head told him something else: that compromising standards was a poor rationalization for the fact that his successful peers ran their practices in a much more businesslike manner than he did. Dental school had little to say about practice management, and Adam mistakenly assumed that that meant that dentistry wasn't a business, a pursuit that he had rejected in the first place.

At long last, Adam came to suspect the hard truth: A better managed practice could mean not only more financial success, but also that he could deliver his high-quality dental care to many more patients. Better management actually would support his goal of quality care. Adam began to see management as a profession, too.

In 1985, Adam decided to learn all that he could about how to better manage his practice. He read articles and books on the subject, attended management seminars, formed a dental management study group with five trusted colleagues who had arrived at similar realizations, and hired a consultant with a stellar track record in the management of dental practices.

With a fresh point of view guiding his way, Adam took a number of important steps to tangibly improve his profitability during the next year. First, he estimated the 10-year horizon of costs and revenues associated with the buy-out of the practice of a nearby dentist who was retiring. Estimating that the net present value of the profit stream of that investment at a fairly conservative 15 percent hurdle rate was $250,000, he obtained a $50,000 note from the bank to buy the practice, and he developed a plan for hiring a staff that would make the new office operate according to his estimates.

Then he started tracking a few key numbers that were among the strongest determinants of his bottom line, profit plus salary: daily revenues attributable separately to him, his hygienists, and to the lab; net new patients each week; weekly collections; and the average age of receivables. He established a policy of greater discipline in staying on schedule from one patient to the next, and he announced a policy of charging no-shows $35. Within a few months, he observed an increase in the number of patients treated daily and in the corresponding profitability numbers.

He also did something he would never have dared to consider only two years earlier: He sent out a flyer to all of the residential zip code addresses in the vicinity of his offices, offering a cleaning and check-up at a special introductory price to help build up his primary practice. Each mailing cost him $1500, but netted him an estimated $15,000 in additional profits over just a 1-year horizon.

By the end of 1986, Adam found that the total of his salary plus net profit improved from $50,000 to $135,000. Equally important, he discovered that he was able to give the same high standard of dental care to twice as many people. Becoming a better businessman has allowed Adam to be a more professional dentist.

A KEY TO SMALL BUSINESS SUCCESS: HOW LONG IT TAKES TO LEARN WHICH NUMBERS TO FOCUS ON

Businesses are often launched by people who have little experience in management. Many have no experience whatever in financial management. They start their businesses because they know a particular skill or market pretty well: interior design, software, health food, newspaper reporting, dentistry, auto repair, advertising, or what have you. They often combine this element of expertise with a degree of confidence that flies in the face of the hard truth about small businesses: Most don't survive beyond a few years. Those who manage the minority of companies that have survived usually came to realize the importance of financial management before it was too late.

At some point, often after a few brushes with financial calamity, people responsible for the business start to think like businesspeople. Usually, they learn first how to manage cash. Then, often because of pressure imposed by investors, they learn to focus on the bottom line of the income statement, and to work their way up the statement to get a sense of why things turned out the way they did. They discover that when they set revenue and cost targets and then hustle to meet them, profits are more likely to show up on the bottom line. And that their instincts about new investment opportunities tend to be more reliable when their ideas can be supported by the numbers.

Those who master this technology develop an ability to consistently steer their companies away from disaster; this is not primarily a matter of luck. Many come to experience both professional and financial success. A few become major contributors to the economy and to society. Remember, all large corporations have their roots in a small business.

13

A FEW WORDS ON BEHALF OF FINANCIAL BEAN COUNTERS

A businessman's judgment is no better than his information.

—R. P. LAMONT

The corporation has publicly taken its lumps for a variety of sins: the sacrifice of quality for profit; preoccupation with short-term financial results at the expense of long-term growth; elevation of the interests of executives over those of stockholders and employees; arrogance; complacency; bigness; and pollution, to name a few. Most of these are, in varying degrees, genuine impediments to the strength of U.S. companies in the world market and to the overall health and well-being of our society.

One criticism of corporate America, however, is misguided and harmful: that our business leaders are preoccupied by the numbers.

Examples of the criticism are numerous. Here's one from Robert Hayes and William Abernathy's widely cited 1980 *Harvard Business Review* article, "Managing Our Way to Economic Decline":

By their preference for servicing existing markets rather than creating new ones and by their devotion to short-term returns and "management by the numbers," many (American managers) have effectively forsworn long-term technological supremacy as a competitive weapon.

David Halberstam advances the Hayes-Abernathy theme in his more recent attack on the "immense power of the finance people" in post-World War II Detroit. A sample from his best-selling 1986 book *The Reckoning*: "The great business schools of America could not produce genius or intuition, but they could and did turn out every year a large number of able, ambitious young men and women who were good at management, who knew numbers and systems, and who knew first and foremost how to minimize costs and maximize profits." He goes on to say that by 1980 most auto industry leaders had become excessively "cautious and finance-oriented."

These portraits of the powerful, yet unimaginative and cautious, fiancial bean counter devoted to short-term returns will hardly attract talented young people to careers in corporate finance. The portraits are, undoubtedly, accurate often enough to persist; but they are cartoons, like that of the slick, Madison-Avenue-hype marketing executive, or the nerdy computer expert. This particular cartoon is typically accompanied by the prescription that U.S. corporations would do much better to follow the example of the Japanese; or that they should be led to a greater degree by people of vision and courage (one of Halberstam's models is Lee Iaccoca); or that they should engage more fully in participatory management, intrapreneuring, or recent developments in the theory of organizational behavior. The skillful use of financial data does not rank high on these lists.

The view that a numbers orientation is somehow closely associated with an obsession for short-term results is especially pernicious. Today's CEO is more likely to have entered the corporate boardroom from a division other than finance, usually the production or marketing division. Those who trade away the company's future for its short-term reported performance, if they've had formal training in finance, didn't learn their lessons about estimating future profit streams and discounting them at appropriate hurdle rates. Myopic executives, regardless of their financial training, tend not to stay there for long. Even mediocre executives know that their reputations and fortunes are more likely to be built on the success of their companies over the long haul than on the numbers for a particular quarter.

Financially skilled executives are, in truth, about like other corporate executives. The best—like Harold Geneen, former chief executive of ITT, and Walter Wriston, former CEO of Citicorp—are second to none. They can be inspiring leaders, creative geniuses, visionaries, team builders, tough competitors, and courageous takers of the calculated risk. And the worst are about like other bad executives.

Whether destined to become the CEO or not, the financial executive in virtually every large, successful corporation provides information that is indispensable to the company: information about which aspects of the business contribute most to the bottom line and which detract from it the most; which investment alternatives are likely to contribute most to the firm's long-term profitability; and which financial instruments are the least expensive to pay for growth, replace assets, and maintain cash balances at levels that preserve the firm's solvency. Consistently successful corporations can do without financial executives and their numbers about as easily as commercial jets can do without navigators and their flight plans.

If financial executives deserve contempt, it is for a different set of sins: bending to pressure to give the boss numbers that support a sentimental favorite course of action; ignoring the effects of intangibles (like the value of management's relations with the staff, and the company's relations with the community) on the bottom line; and analyzing long-term investment alternatives primarily on the basis of simple but shortsighted methods, like the paycheck period criterion, rather than more rigorous methods, like the net present value and internal rate of return criteria.

To their credit, most large companies have not given in to bean-counter bashing to any harmful degree. Financial executives are less likely to become CEOs today than 10 years ago, but their work is used by Fortune 1000 corporations more extensively than ever for management purposes. Why? Primarily because investors and competitors have never been more sophisticated; corporations today have no choice but to base a wide range of critical management decisions on sound data and solid financial analysis.

Of course, no company can be managed by the numbers alone. Nor can a company that emphasizes the wrong numbers —revenues rather than profits, for example—expect to survive for long. But it really is time to lend a little more public respectability to financial analysis and the increasing contribution that it makes to corporate management.

14

MANAGING BY THE NUMBERS: A SUMMARY OF THE ESSENTIALS

Real power has fullness and variety. It is not narrow like lightning, but broad like light.

—ROSWELL D. HITCHCOCK

There is no single path to profitability. Managers who wish to contribute to the profits of their companies can do so in a variety of ways.

One thing is clear: Profitability begins with commitment and understanding. This can be expressed as our first, and perhaps most important, principle.

1. The technology of profit making. There is a technology of profit making; to the degree that it is consciously applied to an organization's operations, the orgnization will tend to be more profitable.

Most people in business want their firms to be profitable, but profit is widely viewed as "what turns up after we exercise good business judgment and work hard, after the people in the accounting department sort out all the data." Those who run

223

businesses that are consistently profitable do more than exercise good judgment, do more than work hard, more than review conventional accounting reports. They operate directly out of a context of profitability; they learn what contributes to profits and what diminishes them, and they purposefully do more of the former and less of the latter.

They can't do so consciously without first having set up a financial guidance system that quickly tells them when and where they're departing from the path of profitability. Which brings us to Power-in-Numbers principle #2:

2. The power of profit-oriented financial data. The firm can improve both its financial performance and its financial condition by creating information that specifically supports its goal of improving profitability.

Generally accepted accounting principles specify accounting conventions that apply to external financial reports rather than to the firm's internal management needs. The consistently profitable firm usually relies primarily on different information —information that enables it to monitor its profitability and to modify its operations quickly as the need becomes apparent.

This does not mean that the firm's financial accounting system should be replaced with one that focuses primarily on internal management needs. It does mean augmenting the financial accounting system with a system that provides information serving internal management needs: budgeting, costing, pricing, inventory control, production scheduling, and decision-making in a variety of areas, such as whether to discontinue an existing product or service line, whether to make or buy a needed product component, and how to finance the purchase of additional assets.

3. The power of segment reporting. The firm enhances its overall profitability when it provides financial information by profit and cost center to the individuals in the firm who hold themselves accountable for maximizing the profits (or controlling costs, when the segment receives no revenue) in each center.

By dividing the organization into profit and cost centers and holding one person accountable for the profits (or costs) of each center, with sound financial data made available to each, the profits for the organization as a whole are generally greater. This does *not* mean that each and every profit center should maximize profit in the current period; an individual profit or cost center may frequently incur additional costs to support greater profits for the organization as a whole, either in the current period or over the longer term. It does mean that doing more of what is profitable and less of what isn't requires that the firm categorize its operations along fairly detailed logical entities—product or service lines, divisions, branches, regions, and so on—and provide financial information that permits each entity to monitor its performance and adapt its operations as needed.

4. The income statement as a power tool for analysis. The income statement can provide crucial information about the firm's success in achieving profitability in three major areas: increasing revenues, increasing the profit margins on goods and services sold, and controlling operating expenses.

The firm can monitor and improve its performance in each of those areas by tracking revenue changes over time, and by tracking the two primary cost categories—cost of goods sold (or cost of sales) and operating expenses—as percentages of revenues over the same time periods. Each of these categories is controlled, in turn, by monitoring each component of the category, such as the direct labor component of the cost of goods sold category and the general and administrative component of the operating expenses category.

5. The balance sheet as a power tool for analysis. The balance sheet becomes comes a useful management tool when it is used to track changes in the firm's assets and the way those assets are financed.

Because asset values reported on the balance sheet tend to diverge from market values over time, the balance sheet is useful primarily for monitoring short-term changes in the firm's capital assets and its debt and equity. Tracking changes in the firm's revenue-producing assets can ensure that the firm's longer-term plans for profitable growth, for phase-out of obsolete equipment, and for improved operating efficiency are in fact being carried out over shorter milestones. Tracking changes in its long-term debt and equity generally enhances the firm's ability to control its financing costs through periodic review of its sources of capital.

6. The power of leverage. Profitable firms make effective use of both debt and equity; their managers understand the advantages and disadvantages of increasing the firm's debt-to-equity ratio.

Just as leverage in physics means getting more work done from less application of force, financial leverage means getting more profit out of the firm's equity by matching the equity, at least in part, with debt to purchase additional profit-producing assets. Financial leverage means making profit for the firm using financial resources from outside the firm, without diluting the existing ownership rights to the firm. More leverage improves the bottom line when the profits attributable to additional debt-financed resources exceed the interest on that debt.

An additional advantage of leverage is that it frequently reduces the corporation's tax burden by substituting interest payments, which are tax deductible, for dividend payments, which are not.

However, because leverage magnifies not only the profits that a given amount of equity can produce, but also magnifies the losses, the firm's managers should carefully work out a reliable plan for creating profits from the additional resources that debt financing makes possible before increasing leverage by incurring debt.

7. *The power of effective planning, control, and budgeting.* *Luck usually plays only a small role in the creation of profits.*

Profits are generally the result of a sequence of steps that begins with the process of stating the firm's business and its goals clearly, and identifying alternative business strategies for achieving those goals. After thoughtfully selecting a strategy, the profit-motivated planner generally turns to those who will execute the plan to develop the details of the plan and an operating budget. Then, control procedures are set up to support those who will execute the plan, and commitments to the plan are obtained from all who have any responsibility for the profits of the firm or any of its parts. When the planning and control process has been conscientiously carried out, executing the plan tends to be straightforward. Variances of actuals from the budgeted amounts are carefully monitored; budget variances provide the signals for corrective action.

8. *The power of profitable pricing.* *Most profitable firms base their prices both on market demand and on inventory replacement costs, not what it paid for the goods.*

The firm's prices are based, in turn, on the prices of competing goods and services, and on reasonable predictions of the behavior of competitors and customers.

Of course, accurate information about market demand, replacement costs, and the future behavior of others tends to be elusive. The costs of estimating those factors are nonetheless worth incurring—up to the point at which the additional cost of refining the estimates begins to exceed the additional profit that can be expected as a result of the refinement. The right pricing level, to borrow Digital Equipment Corporation Chairman Kenneth Olsen's words about decision-making generally, "becomes obvious with hour after hour of working over the details."*

9. The power of profit-oriented investment decisions. *Firms that select investment alternatives that have profit streams with the largest net present values (NPV) will tend to make more profitable investments than firms that focus on other methods for comparing investment alternatives.*

Managers who complain of bad luck are generally those who didn't take the planning process seriously in an earlier period. Such people tend to fly on instinct, which serves most of us pretty well except when the important issues are obscured by complexity. The capital budgeting process—making investment decisions for the firm—is perhaps the clearest case of this. Sound investment decisions involve projections of the future cost and revenue streams associated with each option, and comparisons of the net present values of the resulting profit stream, while taking into account the firm's cost of capital, the risks of each option, depreciation, book and salvage values, the firm's tax bracket, and effects on its other product and service lines and on employee and community relations. Managers who aim to maximize profits in the current period without working out the implications for future profits in a manner that considers those factors systematically are destined eventually to leave the company and develop a wondrous tale or two about forces beyond their control that limited the financial success of their firm.

* Peter Petre, "America's Most Successful Entrepreneur," *Fortune* (October 27, 1986), p. 27.

10. *The power of an assertive profit mentality.* *The best way to predict the future is to create the future.*

Profits grow directly out of the intention of the firm's managers to run a profitable operation. Experience, hard work, and common sense are extremely helpful. Nothing creates profits, however, like the uncommon sense that is associated with a strong and focused intention to have a profitable business.

15

OF COURSE, BUSINESS IS MORE THAN JUST NUMBERS

Statistics are no substitute for judgment.

—HENRY CLAY

The firm's financial numbers are emphasized too little and too late by many managers. The numbers, however, are only one important aspect of management. Like the value of the map and compass to the navigator and the value of the thermometer and clock to the chef, the value of financial data for the manager is real, but limited. The navigator must choose where to go and how to get there; the cook must choose what to cook and how to prepare it. And the manager must choose what business to manage and how to manage it.

Even after basic decisions are made about the business and how to manage it, the numbers can't run the business for the manager. Comparing the budgeted numbers with the actuals, for example, can provide a signal for action quickly after problems begin to occur; but this process doesn't indicate whether it really is appropriate to take any action yet, nor does it prescribe what action to take, if action is called for.

231

To do that, the manager must probe beneath the numbers to find out what's going on. The data can indicate that profits are down primarily because of changes in revenues, or because of changes in costs. After that the manager should ask whether those changes are short-term aberrations or whether they're of a longer-term nature, and why.

Suppose the problem is primarily on the revenues side. Are sales down because of changes in the competition's prices relative to ours? Or because of changes in the quality of the product or service? Or advertising? Are sales down throughout the industry? In light of the answers to those questions, what ideas do our marketing people have about how to improve sales?

Suppose the problem is primarily on the costs side. Are costs up primarily because of changes in our vendors' prices or because of our operating expenses? If the former, can we do better with other vendors? If the latter, which operating expenses are up? What value does the business obtain by incurring each of those costs? Are there less costly ways of receiving the same value? Are all of our overhead items really needed?*

So if the numbers can't answer such fundamental questions, why should managers bother with them? For the same reasons that navigators and cooks bother with tools for measuring their progress. The numbers don't tell managers the whole story, but they do provide the most definitive early warning system known to business, the indispensable first sign of the need for corrective action, and a powerful basis for weighing alternative courses of future action. They are, in short, an essential tool for managing.

---

* Harold Geneen, on scrutinizing "essential" costs: "It is simply amazing how many expenses once deemed necessary become luxuries when your company is operating at a loss." *Managing* (Garden City, NY: Doubleday, 1984), p. 190.

GLOSSARY

Absorption pricing. A method of pricing goods or services based on costs, in which all of the firm's overhead costs are apportioned into the price of the good or service; also known as full cost pricing.

Accelerated Cost Recovery System (ACRS). A depreciation method created by the Economic Recovery Tax Act of 1981 that allows property to be depreciated for tax purposes over shorter terms than those previously in existence. Under ACRS, an asset's life is either 3, 5, 10, or 15 years; depreciable real property can be depreciated over 15 years; and salvage value is ignored in the computation of depreciation.

Accelerated depreciation. A depreciation method whereby the amount of depreciation in the early years of an asset is typically larger than in the later years. For an important exception, see **Accelerated cost recovery system.**

Account payable. An amount owed to another, usually a supplier of goods or services.

Account receivable. An amount due from another, usually the result of a sale of goods or services.

Accrual basis. An accounting method whereby revenues and costs are recognized in the firm's financial records regardless of whether the cash associated with the transaction has been received or paid.

Acid test ratio. An indicator of a firm's short-term solvency. The ratio of its current assets other than inventory to its current liabilities.

Amortization. The systematic writing off or reducing some amount of money for a particular period of time; while depreciation is, technically, a form of amortization, amortization has come to be associated specifically with the writing off of an intangible asset with an expected life of at least one year.

Asset. A resource of the firm.

Average collection period. An indicator of a firm's ability to convert accounts receivable into cash quickly. The ratio of the firm's average accounts receivable to its average daily revenues.

Average payables period. An indicator of a firm's ability to delay the payment of its current liabilities. The ratio of the firm's average accounts payable to its average daily cost of goods sold.

Balance sheet. The statement that reports the primary aspects of a firm's financial condition, in terms of its major categories of assets, liabilities, and capital accounts; sometimes called the statement of financial position.

Book value. The amount of an asset, liability, or equity account reported in the firm's financial record; for a fixed asset, the book value is equal to the asset's purchase cost less the depreciation or amortization that has accumulated for the asset to date.

Bottom line. Net profit after taxes, the last number on the income statement. Colloquially, any ultimate result or goal.

Breakeven analysis. A method of estimating the number of units of a good or service that must be sold at a particular price in order for the firm to at least break even in the production of the item.

Breakeven point. The sales volume (in units or dollars) at which total revenues equal total costs.

Budget. A financial plan, stated in terms of expected or targeted revenues and costs.

Capital. Ownership interest, or the value thereof. See **Net worth.**

Capital budgeting. The process of determining how to allocate limited financial resources among competing investment prospects, prospects whose lives exceed one year.

Capital investment. An expenditure of funds for new plant, machinery, or other asset that produces revenues over a period of at least a year.

Capitalize. To record an expenditure as a fixed asset rather than as an expense.

Cash. A balance sheet item consisting of currency and coin, and savings and checking account balances.

Cash basis. An accounting method whereby revenues and costs are recognized only to the extent that the cash associated with the transaction has been received or paid.

Cash budget. A projection of all cash receipts and outlays expected during a budget period.

Cash flow. An amount of cash generated or consumed by a firm or entity within the firm; the dynamics of cash balances. In analyzing investment opportunities, cash flow refers to the sum of net profit after taxes plus depreciation.

Cash flow statement. A financial report that lists the beginning cash balance, cash receipts and expenditures, and the ending cash balance for a past or future period.

Common stock. The basic ownership entity of a corporation, with each unit represented as a share; all of the corporation's capital stock other than its preferred shares. Common stock has voting rights, but is subordinate to preferred stock with respect to dividends.

Compounding. The process whereby an investment earns interest both on the principal amount of the investment and on the interest earned to date.

Contra account. An account created to write down the value of another account by an appropriate amount.

Control. The process of ensuring that results, especially financial results, coincide with the firm's plans.

Copyright. An intangible asset that gives the holder an exclusive, 28-year right, under federal law, to a specific written work or art object.

Corporation. A legal entity, created by the granting of a charter from an appropriate government authority, and owned by stockholders who have limited liability for the debt of the entity.

Cost. The dollar sacrifice incurred to obtain a product or service; technically, cost refers to the initial sacrifice, while expense refers to the charge against income in a given period.

Cost of goods sold (or cost of sales). The costs that are directly attributable to goods (or services) produced during a specific period of time.

Current asset. An asset to be used up or converted to cash within one year.

Current liability. An obligation to be paid within one year.

Current ratio. An indicator of a firm's short-term solvency. The ratio of its current assets to its current liabilities.

Debt. A financial obligation. See **Liability.**

Debt-to-assets ratio. A measure of a firm's long-term solvency. The ratio of its total liabilities to its total assets; indicates the proportion of the firm's assets that is financed by debt rather than equity.

Debt-to-equity ratio. A measure of a firm's long-term solvency. The ratio of its total liabilities (or its long-term liabilities) to its equity.

Decision analysis. A technique of analyzing decisions under conditions of uncertainty by identifying alternative courses of action and the range of possible outcomes under each alternative, estimating the probability of each contingency, assigning a value to each possible outcome, and selecting the alternative with the best expected result.

Demand curve. A curve that reflects how much of a good or service will be purchased by consumers at various prices.

Depreciation. The systematic writing off or reducing in value of a tangible asset with an expected life of at least one year.

Direct cost pricing. A method of pricing goods or services based on costs, in which only direct costs and those indirect costs that are closely attributable to the good or service produced are included in the price; also known as "incremental cost pricing."

Discount rate. The interest rate used to reduce the value of a stream of future cash flows when calculating their present value.

Discounting. In pricing policy, the process of marking down the price of a good or service sold. In investment analysis, the process of converting a dollar amount to be received or spent at a particular future time to an equivalent amount in the present.

Dividend. A distribution of corporate earnings to stockholders; may be in the form of cash or additional stock.

Double declining balance (DDB) method. A type of accelerated depreciation calculation method. Under DDB, the depreciation for a given year is computed by applying twice the straight-line depreciation percentage ratio to the asset's remaining book value.

Earnings per share. A measure of a corporation's profitability from the stockholders' perspective. The ratio of corporate after-tax profit to the number of shares of stock outstanding.

Effectiveness. Performance, without regard to cost or resource input.

Efficiency. Effectiveness per unit of cost or resource input.

Equity. Ownership interest, or the value thereof. See **Net worth.**

Excess capacity. Idle resources within an organization.

Expenditure. Any payment or cash outlay.

Expense. A direct reduction in the firm's income, made in calculating profit on the income statement. A cost incurred during one period that will not benefit the firm in a subsequent period.

Financial condition. The monetary status of a firm at a point in time.

Financial leverage. The potential profitability advantage provided by assets financed through liabilities rather than capital; usually measured by the firm's debt-to-equity ratio.

Financial performance. The monetary success of a firm over a specific time period.

Financial position. The relationships among a firm's assets, liabilities, and capital, reflected in its balance sheet.

Financial statement analysis. Analysis of the data in a firm's financial statements, aimed generally at assessing the firm's profitability, its liquidity or short-term solvency, or its long-term solvency.

First-in first-out (FIFO) method. A method of valuing a firm's inventory whereby the book value of inventory at the end of a period is calculated on the basis of the cost of the oldest items in the inventory.

Fixed asset. An asset with an expected productive life of at least one year.

Fixed cost. A cost that does not vary with the firm's volume of revenues.

Franchise. An intangible asset that gives the owner exclusive right to operate or sell a specific line of products or services in a particular geographical area.

Full cost pricing. A method of pricing goods or services based on costs, in which all of the firm's overhead costs are apportioned into the price of the good or service; also known as absorption pricing.

Funds. Liquid resources, such as cash or working capital. Amounts of money set aside for special purposes.

Future value. The amount of money that results after the principal and compounding of interest have accumulated over a specified number of periods at a given rate of interest per period.

General ledger. Firm's financial data base, organized by account; the source of the information reported on the firm's financial statements.

Generally accepted accounting principles (GAAP). The standards and conventions of accounting that are widely followed by the profession.

Goodwill. The market value of a firm minus its book value; an intangible asset that shows up on a firm's balance sheet only when the firm or some part of it has been purchased for an amount that differs from its book value. Goodwill derives from a variety of factors: the firm's reputation, location, special relationships with customers and vendors, and so on.

Gross margin percentage. Gross profit as a percent of revenues.

Gross profit. Total revenues minus total cost of goods sold; a measure of the firm's profit before operating expenses and income taxes are accounted for.

Hurdle rate. A firm's minimum acceptable rate of return on its investments. The hurdle rate is typically higher than the firm's cost of capital by an amount that reflects a risk premium; the more risk averse the owners, the larger generally will be the difference between the hurdle rate and the firm's cost of capital.

Income statement. The statement that reports the primary aspects of a firm's financial performance, in terms of its revenues, costs of sales, and its operating expenses.

Incremental cost pricing. A method of pricing goods or services based on costs, in which only direct costs and those indirect costs that are closely attributable to the good or service produced are included in the price; also known as direct cost pricing.

Insolvency. The inability to pay debts with available resources.

Intangible asset. A fixed asset that has no physical existence, such as goodwill, copyrights, franchises, patents, and trademarks.

Internal rate of return (IRR). The effective annual return on investment over the life of a project; the interest rate that sets the net present value of the project's yields equal to the amount of initial investment in the project.

Inventory. A firm's stock of raw materials, work in progress, and goods on hand for sale; a current asset.

Inventory turnover rate. A financial ratio that reflects a firm's liquidity. The ratio of the cost of goods sold to the average inventory value during a period.

Investment. Assets purchased with the specific expectation that they will either yield income or appreciate in value; on the balance sheet, an investment refers to securities of other companies.

Investment audit. A comparison of the actual results of an investment with the estimated results, for the purpose of improving subsequent investment decisions.

Last-in first-out (LIFO) method. A method of valuing a firm's inventory whereby the book value of inventory at the end of a period is calculated on the basis of the cost of the most recent items in the inventory.

Leverage. See **Debt-to-equity ratio, Financial leverage.**

Liability. A financial obligation created from a transaction; requires the eventual payment of cash, goods, or services.

Liquidity. A firm's short-term solvency; its ability to meet current obligations to pay.

Long term. In accounting, a period of at least one year.

Market value. The price at which an item can be sold.

Marketable securities. Securities that can be readily sold at current market prices; a current asset.

Markup. The differential between the price of a good or service and its cost to the firm.

Net income. Excess of revenues over expenses. See **Profit.**

Net present value (NPV). A measure useful for comparing investment alternatives; each alternative is rated by measuring the present value of the investment's profit or cash flow for each period projected, based on a given discount rate, and then totaling the present value amounts for all the periods in the projection.

Net profit. See **Profit.**

Net worth. Total assets minus total liabilities. The equity or capital value of a firm.

Operating budget. A financial statement that documents revenues and expenses planned for a future period.

Operating expenses. The expenses that a firm incurs regardless of the volume of its revenues. Operating expenses include selling expenses and administrative expenses.

Opportunity cost. Profits related to an investment prospect that are foregone by the commitment of assets to another project.

Optimization model. An analytic tool that determines the best (i.e., least cost or maximum yield) allocation of the organization's resources.

Owners' equity. See **Net worth.**

Partnership. An association of two or more persons for the purpose of conducting a business. Partners, unlike the shareholders of a corporation, are fully liable for the debts of the partnership, regardless of their respective equity contributions.

Patent. An intangible asset that gives the holder an exclusive, 17-year right to use a specific process or make a specific product.

Payable. An obligation to another. See **Account payable.**

Penetration pricing. The practice of setting a lower price for a good or service with the hope of discouraging competition and thus attaining greater profits over the long run.

Periodic inventory method. An inventory valuation method whereby the inventory cost is calculated as the beginning inventory, based on physical count, plus purchases, minus the ending inventory.

Perpetual inventory method. An inventory valuation method whereby the inventory value is calculated as the beginning inventory plus purchases minus withdrawals.

Planning. The process of formulating a program to accomplish a specific purpose or goal.

Preferred stock. A class of corporate stock that has no voting rights, but is superior to common stock with respect to rights to dividends.

Present value. The current worth of a specific amount of money to be received at a specific future date, given a particular interest rate.

Price-earnings ratio. The ratio of the current market price of a corporation's stock to its earnings per share.

Pro forma financial statements. Hypothetical future financial statements, based on estimates of the firm's future financial performance.

Profit. The amount that remains during a time period after the costs of sales, operating expenses, and income taxes are subtracted from revenues and interest income; the bottom line of the income statement.

Profit and loss statement. See **Income statement.**

Profit center. A department, regional operation, product or service line, or other aspect of an organization to which revenue and controllable or proportionate costs can be assigned.

Profit range. The range of prices for a good or service within which the firm at least breaks even in producing and marketing it.

Profitability index. The present value of net cash inflows divided by the net cash outlays.

Proprietorship. A business owned by one person.

Quick ratio. See **Acid test ratio.**

Rate of return. Profit per dollar of investment.

Receivable. A financial claim against another, with a specific amount due to be received. See **Account receivable.**

Regression analysis. A statistical method for estimating the line that best predicts the values of one variable (such as total revenue for the next fiscal year) based on the values of one or more other variables (such as time, expressed in prior years, advertising expenditures in each prior year, and so on).

Replacement cost (or value). The current cost of reproducing an asset or its function. For the purpose of pricing based on costs, replacement costs provide a more profitable basis than do the historical costs that show up on the firm's income statements.

Reserve. An amount set aside in anticipation of likely future costs.

Retained earnings. A firm's accumulated profits at a point in time—specifically, those that are reinvested in the firm rather than paid out to the owners of the firm; an equity account on the balance sheet.

Return on stockholders' equity. A measure of a corporation's profitability from the prospective of the stockholders. The ratio of aftertax profit to the average stockholders' equity during a period.

Return on investment (ROI). A measure of the earnings from an investment. Usually expressed as an annualized percentage, ROI is the ratio of the earnings to the initial outlay.

Revenue. The firm's proceeds or income from the sale of goods or services.

Robinson-Patman Act. A law passed in 1936 making it illegal to charge two different prices for a given good or service to two different customers in such a way that lessens competition.

Security. A financial instrument, such as stock shares or bonds, that represents ownership or rights to interest in an institution.

Segment reports. Financial reports that show financial data by a component of the business—a product or service line, department or division, branch, etc.

Selling expense. An operating expense associated with the marketing and distribution of a firm's goods or services.

Short term. In accounting, a period of up to one year.

Simulation model. A mathematical representation of a real-world resource allocation problem, designed to test the effects of alternative allocations of an organization's resources on performance.

Sinking fund. The amount of each deposit in a series of interest-drawing deposits needed to yield a particular amount in the future.

Skimming. The practice of setting the price of a new product or service at a higher than normal markup when it first emerges on the market, and gradually lowering it as competition emerges, in order to receive the higher prices that a smaller number of customers are willing to pay for the new item.

Solvency. The ability to pay debts with available resources as they become due.

Statement of changes in financial position. A financial statement that reports the sources and uses of liquidity, cash or working capital, during an accounting period.

Stockholders' equity. The total book value amount of ownership interest in a corporation.

Straight-line depreciation. A simple depreciation method whereby the depreciation amount in each period is equal to the initial book value of the asset divided by the number of periods over which the asset is depreciated.

Strategic plan. A long-term plan shaped with special awareness of external, difficult to control factors such as likely behavior of the competition, the economy, consumers, suppliers, and employees.

Sum-of-the-years'-digits method. A type of accelerated depreciation method in which a steadily decreasing fraction of an asset's depreciable cost is written off each year.

Supply curve. A curve that reflects how much of a good or service will be made available to consumers by providers at various prices.

Tax avoidance. The arrangement of the financial affairs of a taxpayer, either an individual or business, such that the taxpayer's income taxes are legitimately reduced.

Tax evasion. The willful and fraudulent withholding of taxes from a government.

Trademark. An intangible asset that gives the holder the exclusive and continuing right to use specific names or symbols to identify a brand or family of products.

Transaction. Any financial activity or event that is recorded in the firm's general ledger.

Transfer price. The price set for a good or service that is sold from one division or subsidiary to another within a larger enterprise.

Vertical integration. The practice of a firm's producing its own raw materials or services, usually with the intention of doing so at a lower cost than it would otherwise have to bear if it paid for them in the open market.

Working capital. The difference between a firm's current assets and its current liabilities; a measure of the firm's liquidity cushion.

Write-off (or write-down). A reduction in an asset account due to an abnormal event.

INDEX